The Enduring Legacy

The book outlines the historical, political, and pedagogical reality of growing segregation and racial isolation in America's twenty-first-century public schools. It explores the dialectic between the philosophies of inclusion and exclusion, examining an underlying contradiction: public education that continually postures to be ever more inclusive while simultaneously perpetuating an exclusive system through systematized discrimination to maintain inequality. The book concludes that undoing resegregation is imperative to achieve social justice and a better education for all children.

Mark Ryan has taught at all grade levels from elementary classes to university seminars. He holds a Bachelor of Arts degree in History from the University of California at Santa Cruz, a Master of Education degree from the University of Puerto Rico at Rio Piedras, and a Doctorate in Higher and Adult Education from Arizona State University at Tempe. He was awarded the President's Distinguished Teaching Award at National University. Ryan's best-known work is *Ask the Teacher: A Practitioner's Guide to Teaching and Learning in the Diverse Classroom* (2000, 2001, 2002, 2008). He has co-authored two books with Peter Serdyukov, *Writing Effective Lesson Plans: The 5-Star Approach* (2012) and the *5-Minute Lesson Plan* (2013). His latest book *The Enduring Legacy: Structured Inequality in Americans Schools* (2020), contains a foreword by Secretary Leon Panetta.

The Enduring Legacy

*Structured Inequality in
America's Public Schools*

Mark Ryan

University of Michigan Press
Ann Arbor

For questions or permissions, please contact um.press.perms@umich.edu

Published in the United States of America by the
University of Michigan Press
Manufactured in the United States of America
Printed on acid-free paper
First published September 2020

A CIP catalog record for this book is available from the British Library.

Library of Congress Cataloging-in-Publication Data

Names: Ryan, Mark, 1947– author.
Title: The enduring legacy : structured inequality in America's public schools / Mark Ryan.
Description: Ann Arbor : University of Michigan Press, 2020. | Includes bibliographical
    references and index.
Identifiers: LCCN 2020015668 (print) | LCCN 2020015669 (ebook) | ISBN 9780472074686
    (hardcover) | ISBN 9780472054688 (paperback) | ISBN 9780472127276 (ebook)
Subjects: LCSH: Segregation in education—United States—History. | Discrimination in
    education—United States—History. | Racism in education—United States—History. | Public
    schools—United States—History. | Educational equalization—United States. | Education—
    Political aspects—United States.
Classification: LCC LC212.52 .R93 2020 (print) | LCC LC212.52 (ebook) | DDC 379.2/630973—
    dc23
LC record available at https://lccn.loc.gov/2020015668
LC ebook record available at https://lccn.loc.gov/2020015669

The past is never dead. It's not even past.

—WILLIAM FAULKNER

CONTENTS

Digital materials related to this title can be found on the Fulcrum platform via the following citable URL: https://doi.org/10.3998/mpub.11645040

FIGURES

FOREWORD

The *Enduring Legacy* is a wake-up call for American education to never stop fighting to fulfill the promise that all of our children are entitled to an equal education.

For too long, America's public education has historically provided dual and disparate opportunities and outcomes for its children. From the eighteenth-century common school to the twenty-first-century public school, there has been a struggle between the enlightened forces of inclusion and a tradition of exclusion within American society.

The historical and political record compels a policy imperative: in order to provide a free public education of the highest quality for every child, the growing reality of renewed school segregation must be rejected. A true democracy recommends it, the art of teaching requires it, and the Constitution demands it. Simply put, public schools have been resegregating for decades. We know what the problem is. But why this problem persists needs examination.

One reason for an increasingly separate and unequal public school system is the negligence of scholars in general and schools and colleges of education in particular to tackle this problem effectively. Those who do not directly oppose segregated schools, and tinker with the racial achievement gap by asking more of students, parents, and teachers stuck in segregated schools, misunderstand the legacy of *Brown v. Board of Education*, uphold the false separate-but-equal remnants of *Plessy v. Ferguson*, and are oblivious to the work and goals of Rev. Martin Luther King Jr.

Too much blood has been sacrificed in the fight for equal education to simply accept the consequences of resegregation. I know because I was part of that fight as director of the U.S. Office for Civil Rights in the late 1960s.

Although there were a number of brave education officials and leaders who tried to do the right thing and break up the dual school system, the politics of resistance kept raising its ugly head. Thanks to the federal courts and the many dedicated civil rights attorneys and public servants, the struggle to break down racial barriers in education and enforce the requirement of *Brown v. Board of Education* made significant progress. Many, like myself, lost our jobs in that fight. But the country moved in the right direction because it was right—morally, legally, and educationally. And as Mark Ryan makes clear in this book, it is our job to continue that progress and never retreat from the promise of equal education.

Although no single educational policy can change the legacy of structured inequality in the American public school, a balanced mix of clear policies, programs, and practices based on what has worked in the past, coupled with new technologies of what may be effective in the future, is needed. Teacher education programs are in dire need of curricular change to prepare today's teacher candidates for the continuing reality of the segregated public school classroom. In particular, these programs must provide new teachers with the awareness, knowledge, and cultural competence to begin to transform public schools from islands of racial isolation to welcoming places of inclusion.

The key to success rests in strong political and educational leadership. There must be a commitment to equal education in the political, judicial, and educational arenas.

A free public education that provides an equal opportunity for all children is more than an American ideal. It is the very foundation of our democracy. Historic cracks in that foundation grow wider each day. That is because our educational system, which routinely hails inclusion, mostly is accepting of exclusion. New approaches and a willingness to pursue fairness for every child by combating segregation is not just a noble cause. It is the professional responsibility of every teacher, principal, superintendent, college professor, and dean. It is the duty of every citizen and elected leader who pledges loyalty to the Constitution. Where inequality exists, it makes all of us less equal. The education of our children and indeed the future of our democracy are at stake.

LEON E. PANETTA

FORMER DIRECTOR OF THE U.S. OFFICE FOR CIVIL RIGHTS

PREFACE

Enduring Legacy describes a multifaceted historical, political, and pedagogical paradox—a constant struggle between those who consistently espouse a message of hope and inclusion and others who systematically plan for the layered hierarchies of exclusion. At the core of this book is the description of structured inequality in the nation's schools that is deeply connected to social stratification within American society. This paradox is viewed through a chronological lens that began in the eighteenth century and has provided an enduring legacy into the twenty-first century. The practical aspect of this book is to provide a historical, political, and pedagogical context for teacher candidates not only to comprehend the nature of racial segregation but as future educators understand their professional responsibility both in the community and in the school to strive for an integrated classroom where all children are given a chance to succeed. The goal of providing every child a world-class education is not only an ethical imperative, it is an inherent necessity for a functioning pluralistic democracy. The challenge is both great and growing, for teachers today will face an American classroom ever more segregated in the 2020s.

Since the very foundation of the Republic, Americans rich and poor, black and white, male and female have received qualitatively different educational opportunities.[1] The historic quest for a more egalitarian model embodies the warp and woof of positive social change in public schools, for it goes to the heart of whether public education provides a fundamentally inclusionary or exclusionary function within the nation. There is much evidence via a historical examination of these two deeply held polarizing beliefs. The dueling philosophies of inclusion and exclusion both emanate from a web of intensely held yet contradictory views of the American experience.[2] The inclusionary vision embraces a vibrant democracy, an educated citizenry, and concomitant personal and societal improvement.[3] On the contrary, the exclusionary view imagines a type of intellectual meritocracy—a traditional bio-societal totem pole justified via the use of statistical data to effectively categorize society into a layered hierarchy. Typical public school mission statements articulate a dynamic faith in an inclusive learning process, seen as vital to a participatory democracy, which can be traced to the beginnings of the American Republic.[4] Nevertheless, there is an opposite and also genuinely American view—that of exclusion. It grew out of the eighteenth- and nineteenth-century ideas of racial superiority, and was then adapted into philosophical notions such as Social Darwinism and later promoted and institutionally implemented by means of human intelligence test-based findings in the twentieth and twenty-first centuries. The traditional belief in the inevitability of social stratification is one of the historical antecedents perpetuating the prevalence of structured inequality that continues to this day to promote defined academic tracks (e.g., perceived ability grouping) in the American classroom.[5] Accordingly, from de jure and so-called de facto segregation to I.Q. rankings and standardized evaluations, to long-standing linkages between schooling and property values, the notion of exclusion to limit or effectively bar access to public education appears to have been implemented methodically over the last century.[6]

To better understand the phenomena of social stratification and its philosophic underpinnings, this book has three parts. Part 1 presents a historical analysis that examines the enduring legacy of past structured inequality. Part 2 is a consideration of the relationship between political power an educational policy with a special emphasis on the Southern Strategy, an explicit plan used since the mid-1960s by conservatives to gain political support in the former Confederate states in the South by appealing to traditional racist animus against African Americans. Part 3 is a pedagogic exploration of the fundamental flaw of structured inequality in the American educational system. In addition, there is a consideration of solutions that embrace constructive change in the classroom by implementing models of genuine inclusion, based on equality and equity for America's twenty-first-century schools. It is this author's intent, within the historic dialectic between the philosophies of inclusion and exclusion, to examine an underlying contradiction: public education that continually postures to be ever more inclusive while simultaneously perpetuating an exclusive system through systematic discrimination that maintains and even exacerbates inequality.

The public school is the last great meeting place of American democracy. Teacher candidates and the professors in teacher education programs in colleges and universities across the nation cannot afford to be ignorant or apathetic about the growing resegregation in America's classrooms. What is called for is a knowledge of the historical, political, and pedagogical reality that functions as an environment of structured inequality. To those who ask, "Where does American education go from here?," we must first understand where we are. The segregated school is a decaying building on a dead-end street. For a growing number of teachers and students that run-down edifice is precisely where we are. There is no Global Positioning System in the world that can tell us where we are going if we do not know where we are.

ACKNOWLEDGMENTS

Toni Morrison once wrote that "if there's a book that you want to read, but it hasn't been written yet, then you must write it." So, let me acknowledge so many of my graduate students who encouraged me to write a book to match our online discussions of the future schools we want to see in the United States. This multifaceted text that approaches the archetypal notions of inclusion and exclusion via an analysis of historical, political, and pedagogical realties could not have been written alone. Such a daunting task required the assistance and inspiration of some very special professionals. First, I would like to thank my editor, Elizabeth Demers, senior acquisitions editor, at the University of Michigan Press, who guided my manuscript though a rigorous peer-review process. I would also like to express my gratitude to Peter Serdyukov and Nilsa Thoros whose valuable counsel helped guide the text through its formative stages. In addition, many thanks to Matthew Laubacher for his counsel about both the style and substance of the final manuscript. Finally, I am indebted to Secretary Leon Panetta, who penned the foreword of *Enduring Legacy*, and whose distinguished career of service to our nation as secretary of defense, director of the CIA, White House chief of staff, and Congressman from California is among the most heralded of any person in American history. More germane for this book, however, was the secretary's principled action when confronted with the directives of President Nixon who, as part of his Southern Strategy, desired a *lack* of enforcement of equal education laws in order to protect his political standing among Southern white voters. Secretary Panetta, as the then director of the Office of Civil Rights, resigned at age thirty-one in 1970, rather than accede to such policies. Such noble and selfless action then as now is more than laudable; it is necessary to challenge the half century of growing racial isolation from the 1970s to the 2020s in America's classrooms.

PART 1
A Historical Analysis

Figure 1. Students saying the Pledge of Allegiance at the Weill Public School in San Francisco in 1942. Those of Japanese descent later were sent to relocation centers for the duration of the war.

A Struggle between Forces

The traditional belief in the inevitability of social stratification via class, gender, and race is one of the historical antecedents perpetuating the prevalence of structured inequality in today's American classroom. The history of public education in the United States may be viewed as a constant struggle between the forces of those who consistently espouse a message of hope and inclusion and others who systematically plan for the layered hierarchies of exclusion. Promoting the common good via public schools by strengthening participatory democracy via an educated citizenry has become, over time and trials, a deeply held American conviction that reflects the nation's core values.[1] Adlai Stevenson once observed in the middle of the twentieth century that "the most American thing about America is the free common school system."[2] The remark was surely meant to applaud the idea of a free public school—a shared expectation of an academy where every citizen is accepted and American democracy is celebrated. Yet today, just as in the Pledge of Allegiance with the oft-recited egalitarian promise of "liberty and justice for all," the assurance of an equal educational opportunity for every citizen remains not only an unfulfilled goal, but one that is in danger of becoming little more than sanctimonious rhetoric. Viewed from the reality of public education at present, a more conflicted (if unintended) yet more historically accurate meaning may be gleaned from Stevenson's remark.

America's public schools are presently undergoing a process of resegregation to the point that they are more segregated today than they were at any point in the last 40 years.[3] Even in integrated schools, structured inequality routinely occurs via perceived ability grouping. Today, tracking (i.e., separating students into rigid homogenous groups based on a student's perceived ability) is widespread in American public schools.

Tracking or ability grouping is a practice of grouping children together according to their "talents" in the classroom. The practice is ubiquitous across the United States. Based on perceived ability and other factors, schools (e.g., teachers, counselors, and administrators) group students into so-called remedial, regular, and advanced groups.[4] The remedial and regular groups uniformly received a less demanding academic curriculum than the advanced students. The rationale is based on the following assumptions. First, students' intellectual differences are so great that a common curriculum would either slow down the higher-tracked students or hopelessly confuse the lower-tracked students. Second, students learn more grouped with those of similar ability. Third, lower-track students develop better attitudes when they are not grouped with higher-track students. Fourth, students are divided into relatively high academic and low academic groups via a fair method. Fifth, teachers find it easier to individualize instruction in homogeneous groups. The problem is that none of these assumptions are research based—and in fact there has long been much scholarly evidence to prove that tracking is harmful to many students.[5]

Remedial classes historically do not remediate, nor do compensatory classes compensate.[6] What is called for instead of tracking is to teach the most enriched curricula to all students via the widest variety of methodological approaches. In her article "Detracking in Social Studies: A Path to a More Democratic Education?," Nora Hyland stated that "content goals and the pedagogical orientations of social studies classes lend themselves to detracking." She also noted that pedagogical practices recommended for teaching social studies are likewise implemented in successful detracked classrooms.[7] There can be little question that the differences in the course-specific tracks students take (e.g., advanced, regular, or remedial offerings) across the curricula, especially in math, science, and foreign language, have a profound impact on student scores in the current high-stakes-testing environment. It has long been known and hardly surprising that the more rigorous the curriculum a learner is exposed to, the greater the opportunity for student achievement and consequently the higher the standardized test score. Those qualifying test results, the product of student work based to a great extent on exposure to enriched curricular content and concepts, can virtually open or close the door to higher education. Who succeeds and who is left behind in today's competitive rankings-based society is subject all too often to a quantitative measure taken on an unbalanced playing field. To understand the practice of structured inequality within the American educational experience demands an examination of traditional perspectives, which continue to guide the public school at the beginning of the twenty-first century.

The history of structured inequality in the nation's schools has been deeply connected to social stratification within American society at large.[8] There are various basic themes that can be viewed through a chronological lens that begin in the eighteenth century and provide an enduring legacy into the twenty-first century. First to be studied within the origin of America's ambiguous philosophical roots are democratic values.[9] Those ideals form a foundation of the nation's evolution from the common school to the public school paradigm.[10] Next, the dual nature of inclusionary language and exclusionary tradition will be examined in the segregationist polices reflected through Social Darwinism, white superiority via pseudo empiricism, and the promotion of assimilation by means of Americanism in the classroom. Finally, the personification of this duality—the paradox of promoting inclusion while practicing exclusion—will be viewed through Ellwood Patterson Cubberley (1868–1941). His life and legacy embodied the consequential movement to conceptualize perceived ability grouping, racial superiority, and the enduring legacy of structured inequality. History is not a simple linear narrative. It must be understood that educational inequality is not always the intentional and deliberate work of those who would deny justice to those most marginalized. An accurate history also includes an array of unintended consequences, ignorance, and apathy that also leads down the pathway of racist ideas, policies, and practices.

An Ambiguous Philosophical Root

Although the contemporary public school, a direct descendent of the common school, is supported via property taxes, tuition free, open to all children, and state regulated with day-to-day local control of local school boards, the philosophical root of the public school goes back to the eighteenth century. Benjamin Franklin wrote in 1749, "The good Education of Youth has been esteemed by wise Men in all Ages, as the surest Foundation of the Happiness both of private Families and of Common-wealths."[11] It was Thomas Jefferson who in 1778 proposed to the Virginia Assembly "A Bill for the More General Diffusion of Knowledge" (subsequently voted down three times between 1779 and 1817). The bill promoted the concept of education that aimed to provide a natural aristocracy for the American experiment in democracy. Jefferson (1814) promoted a two-tiered educational system, with different tracks for "the laboring and the learned."[12] Moreover, the Jeffersonian vision of the common school, universal free education of every (white) boy for three years, and then a university education for the elite of this group, was revolutionary for the times: "By this means twenty of the best geniuses will be raked from the rubbish annually and be instructed at the public expense."[13] Significantly, Jefferson's ideas are a product of a conflicted American sociopolitical reality. Jefferson was a slave owner (said to own over 200 slaves) who at the same time believed in individual freedom and a type of national intellectual meritocracy.

Figure 2. Benjamin
Franklin as depicted
in a 1780 engraving.

Figure 3. An 1805
engraving of Thomas
Jefferson.

During Jefferson's lifetime slavery was sustained by brutal force. Unlike many other Virginia landowners, Jefferson never freed his slaves. He seemed quite willing to profit off the bondage of others. Ibram X. Kendi posited that racism does not emanate alone from mere ignorance or blind hatred. Instead, it is also used as a justification to segregate and provide a rationale for inequities.[14] Of course, it is obvious that the benefactors of those inequities were and are those in positions of power. One of Jefferson's slaves was Sally Hemmings. DNA studies by the Jefferson Foundation, along with documentary and statistical evidence, showed a high probability that Thomas Jefferson was most likely the father of Sally Hemings's six children.[15]

Jefferson's dual nature is an American enigma. Here was a man who wrote passionately about liberty and independence—who nevertheless had a personal socioeconomic acceptance of slavery, a practice that excluded an entire race of people (estimated at 20 percent of the American population at that time) from the benefits of liberty—and the educational opportunities needed to represent and sustain a participatory democracy for all people. Jefferson was conflicted over the matter of race and presents a pedagogical argument on its corrupting influence:

> There must doubtless be an unhappy influence on the manners of our people produced by the existence of slavery among us. The whole commerce between master and slave is a perpetual exercise of the most boisterous passions, the most unremitting despotism on the one part, and degrading submissions on the other. Our children see this and learn to imitate it; for man is an imitative animal. This quality is the germ of all education in him.[16]

Revolutionary for the time, yet divisive in nature, Jefferson's twin schoolhouse ideals—a more inclusive brand of universal education and the inherently exclusive aforementioned notion that "geniuses will be raked from the rubbish"—are an expression of classic American pedagogical contradictory dualism. While spreading the first glimmer of hope and inclusion for some who had been traditionally shut out of a formal education (able white men), it is notable that his utopian vision did not include the same opportunities for women (there was a three-year limit to school for girls). Correspondingly, consistent with Jefferson's practice of holding slaves (which he considered a form of moral depravity), people of color were not considered for formal schooling of any kind; indeed, it was among the gravest offenses to teach African Americans to read and write. For example, antiliteracy laws in antebellum Georgia gave official approval to illiteracy, as those decrees were meant to calm the worst fears concerning the power of educated African Americans.[17] Thus, the concept of individual freedom in the reality of the late eighteenth century excluded the majority of the American population and was restricted to freedom for certain white male individuals.

In many ways, Jefferson's plea for more schooling embodies a reoccurring schizophrenia in the American view of education. This kind of duality in the American experience has also been noted by Ibram X. Kendi. He posited there is no singular movement on the issue of racism, but two distinct historical forces proclaiming equality and decreeing inequality. So it is now and so it was then with Jefferson. Although a slave owner, there is the clear impulse for the hopeful notion of inclusion—the egalitarian side of the Jeffersonian duality of mind promoting education for all "without regards to wealth, birth, or accidental condition."[18] It is an argument that rhetorically soars in the laudatory quest for an informed democracy. Correspondingly, Jefferson's writings are replete with the stated conviction that democracy can best function with an educated citizenry. In an 1816 letter to Colonel Charles Yancy, Jefferson intoned, "If a nation expects to be ignorant and free, in a state of civilization, it expects what never was and never will be."[19] Notwithstanding Jefferson's eloquent analysis of the imperative nature of public education in the securing and maintaining of liberty, one is also presented with the dehumanizing exclusionary image of clearing away the "rubbish" and, after disposing of trash, presumably producing a new strain of American students to become a merit-based elite.[20] While Jefferson's words and practices may seem inconsistent, the unambiguous historical record of exclusion toward all but certain white males begs for a fundamental rationale for those eighteenth-century leaders (e.g., attendees at the Constitutional Convention of 1789) who freely chose to make a distinction between races. Of course, questioning the mind and soul of eighteenth-century leaders—particularly Jefferson—is fraught with issues of time, place, and intention. One must be mindful of the notion of presentism, a bias to interpret of past events using today's twenty-first-century perspectives.

To be historically accurate as to the rationale of America's founding fathers demands a holistic view of that time and place and the genuine intention of founding a republic. No doubt Jefferson's view and stated aim for republican schools was to provide new leaders via formal education that would be both inclusive (to able white men) and hierarchical. Nevertheless, his republicanism can be conceptually viewed in terms of an eighteenth-century sociopolit-

8

ical reality as a merger of the "pursuit of happiness" within the Declaration of Independence with legalized slavery nascent in the Constitution. In Jefferson's case, it could be argued that his opinions were not (solely) based on blind bigotry or the avarice of slave owners, but a far more seductive theory that stems from eighteenth-century study of natural history. Jefferson expresses among his many doubts about race relations a "suspicion" of racial superiority. Thus, among the intelligentsia of that time there was a kind of "naturally" designed discrimination. This type of racism based on empirical observation and naive extrapolation took root early on American soil.

From its very beginning and from its best and brightest intellectuals, there is a tradition in American civic institutions in general and American public education in particular of accepting forms of structured inequality—nurtured in racist, sexist, and classist law and custom that existed and continues to shape and skew society via public schools into the twenty-first century. Such a racial achievement gap has been socially and institutionally constructed. Derrick Darby and John Rury have discussed the societal acceptance of "racial differences" in intellectual ability, moral character, and subsequent behavior promoted by eighteenth-century philosophers, such as David Hume and Immanuel Kant.[21] As we have seen—in that same formative century for the American Republic—Jefferson's similar beliefs on racial superiority influenced his mind-set on the nature of the teaching and learning enterprise. Not surprisingly, strong opposition to so-called racial differences was evidenced in the authentic voices from those who endured lifelong racial bias and animus during the nineteenth and twentieth centuries, including Frederick Douglass, Frances Ellen Watkins Harper, W. E. B. Du Bois, and Thurgood Marshall.

Growing Democratic Values

To both Jefferson and Franklin, the concept of social mobility via self-education was a fundamental value on which to premise the new republic. The Jeffersonian pursuit of happiness envisioned the diffusion of knowledge in an agrarian world. On the other hand, Franklin's public life as an author, inventor, printer, publisher, scientist, and diplomat with a penchant for invention promoted a flow of learning channeled via the world of mechanical technology that "let light into the nature of things, tend[ed] to increase the power of man over matter, and multiply the conveniences and pleasures of life."[22]

Thus, whether it was Jefferson's farmer or Franklin's mechanic, the common man's improvement by means of education was not only seen as laudatory but critical to the health of a democratic nation. The continuous battle to democratize education was later led by immigrants like Timothy Claxton and William Maclure. As they struggled to bring education to the common working man in the early part of the nineteenth century via publications (e.g., *Memoir of a Mechanic*, *The Young Mechanic*) the idea of lifelong education was essential, because "for want of mental cultivation, men do become dupes of those better informed."[23] Correspondingly, the then radical egalitarianism of Maclure led to his notions of social reform via education by way of tax-supported schools. By writing that "knowledge is both power and wealth," Maclure had adopted a tenet of what is now termed critical pedagogy.[24] The growing friction in the early nineteenth century between the schooled and unschooled classes was occurring at a time when knowledge and new technologies were becoming increasingly specialized. For instance, professional societies set stricter admission policies and professional journals of the time gravitated toward a greater lexical density not easily understood by those possessing little if any formal education. In short, exclusion of the common man in the first half of the nineteenth century by the social and intellectual elite was becoming a fait accompli. Even the lyceum movement, which was supposed to promote education for the working class, moved away from practical scientific knowledge to what some have termed "innocuous popular entertainment." Working men of the 1830s rejected the traditional idea of self-improvement for themselves via the concept of useful knowledge, but embraced the inclusive idea of universal common schooling for their children. The notion of free public education—a common school—was ascending. As Sarah Mondale and Sarah Patton noted, during the 1830s through the 1870s, great changes were made in public schooling across the country. The common school movement had three basic goals. First, to afford a free education for white children. Second, to train teachers. Third, using the power under the Tenth Amendment, to establish state control over public schools. Horace Mann championed the second goal of teacher training. Mann stated that education should be provided by well-trained, professional teachers. What began in the nineteenth century was a defining moment in the history of American education. The commencement of education of the masses forwarded by reformers such at Horace Mann and William Holmes McGuffey (his *McGuffey Readers* sold over 120 million copies) paved the way for state-funded public schools.[25]

Hilary Moss has showed the complexity of the common school movement where opposite trends were in conflict. On the one hand, there was the
bold persistence of African Americans who wanted education, while at the
same time there was strong white opposition to those efforts. Further adding
to the complexity of the times, there existed a fractured national map on race.
This was not a stereotypical North-South cultural conflict. White residents of
antebellum Boston and New Haven rejected the education of African Americans in their schools, while city dwellers in slaveholding Baltimore voiced no
strong opposition to the establishment of African American schools. Even
as white enmity to African American education grew, African Americans
reacted to demand public schooling. It was a time when public school expansion and growing white opposition to African American attendance in public
schools were occurring simultaneously.[26]

To maintain segregated schools, new laws were contrived to shut the
schoolhouse door to African Americans. Consider the case of young Sarah
Harris Fayerweather, who aspired to become a teacher. Fayerweather was
allowed to matriculate at Prudence Crandall's all-girls school in Canter-
bury, Connecticut. This marked the first racially integrated schoolhouse in
the nation. Yet her admission directly caused the school's forcible closure
under the Connecticut Black Law of 1833. Legislation was passed through
the Connecticut Assembly outlawing the establishment of schools "for the
instruction of colored persons belonging to other states and countries." African Americans at that time were considered to be noncitizens. Accordingly,
the rationale for public schooling was premised on the notion of citizenship,
not equality.[27]

The Evolution from Common School to Public School

As the American nation developed so did the common school. Of course, this
evolution was not inevitable as America was struggling with its uniqueness
as a nation-state. Carolyn Eastman shows how American society of the late
eighteenth century and early nineteenth century began to evolve a national
identity. This gradual development of the idea enshrined in the Constitution as "we the people" was a muddled process in 1789. Yet slowly through
engaged oratory, education, print media, and schools a definable American
identity slowly melded into more standard views of politics, mores, and manners across diverse sections of the country.[28] Likewise, notions of gender and

Figure 4. An 1870 view of a layered school system eschewing sectarian bitterness and unfair distribution of funds while favoring the idea of a common school.

race relations began to form and take hold, the residue of which we can still identify in modern America.

Given the myriad of influences on culture, schools provided that part of education not replicated by family experience or other institutions such as the church. Schools were then and are now the entry level institution to our values, dreams, and aspirations. Furthermore, schools connected two democratic imperatives: preparing citizens and enabling each individual to enjoy the pursuit of happiness. In a broader sense, public education acculturated the values and norms of a national identity (e.g., the *McGuffey Readers*). In the decades flanked by the American Revolution and the Civil War, as Johann Neem explains, Americans in cities and towns mapped school districts and constructed schoolhouses with the idea of expanding tax support and hiring teachers (many of them women) to offer many children a liberal education. It is not that there was consensus on every educational issue. Debates on funding sources and governance, as they are today, were part of that nineteenth-century reality. Yet, by the 1860s, most of the states in the North had made common schools free, and states in the South were seen as following suit. Education in general and the institution of the school were viewed as a public good. Eventually, and certainly by the end of the Civil War, the American people changed their view on nationhood. Americans went from a mind-set of the United States *are* to the United States *is*. This notion of a collective identity to prepare citizens and foster the idea of one nation was part of the common school legacy. The complex relationship between school and society was also noted by Nancy Beadie, who showed how schools were among the forces that drove the establishment of capital (social, political, and financial) during what she termed as the market revolution and capitalist transition of the early republican era.[29]

American Exceptionalism

John Demos also mentioned the idea of an enduring legacy in our national tradition—the formation of a multifaceted notion—American exceptionalism. On the one hand, it is the idea of the need to reach out to the needy or the stranger with a missionary zeal. On the other hand, this munificence often converted into presumption, arrogance, and even imperialism—in which a feeling of superiority is inevitably embedded. In his book *Heathen Nation*, Demos related a unique missionary project devised by various eminent Protestant ministers to gather children from around the globe and place them in a redemptive setting where, ultimately, they could learn about "civilization" and convert to Christianity. The "heathen youth" would be drawn from all parts of the earth, and would include Native Americans. This experiment eventually failed in part when the issue of racial intermarriage tested the founders' ideals. The familiar voice of racial intolerance silenced the earnest hope of reconciliation.

The boundaries of acceptance and Christian charity in the early nineteenth century had their limits—limits that had lasting power. Accordingly, the plight of Native Americans in the late nineteenth and twentieth centuries was revisited. This time they were removed, not by church leaders but by federal authorities, from their homes and shunted into government boarding schools.[30] Like the Protestant ministers of the early part of the nineteenth century, government policy makers assumed that white ideals that defined "civilization" more than counterbalanced what they deemed to be the Native Americans' inherent "savagism." Retired brigadier general Richard H. Pratt, founder of the Carlisle Indian Industrial at Carlisle, Pennsylvania, noted in in an 1892 speech:

> A great general has said that the only good Indian is a dead one, and that high sanction of his destruction has been an enormous factor in promoting Indian massacres. In a sense, I agree with the sentiment, but only in this: that all the Indian there is in the race should be dead. Kill the Indian in him, and save the man.[31]

The reconstruction was to be both psychological and cultural. In Pratt's full speech, he draws analogies to the "civilizing" of African Americans. While race relations careened toward nationally codified segregation in 1896 in the aftermath of *Plessy v. Ferguson*, women's educational opportunities faced similar bigotry with a distinct history.

What Is the Profession of a Woman?

Catharine Beecher queried in 1829, "What is the profession of a woman?" Her response was that well-educated woman were uniquely suited to the profession of teaching. She noted in that year, "If all females were not only well educated themselves but were prepared to communicate in an easy manner their stores of knowledge to others; if they not only knew how to regulate their own minds, tempers, and habits but how to effect improvements in those around them, the face of society would be speedily changed." The women's movement to promote female teachers was afoot in the mid-nineteenth century as part of a broad social and cultural shift. This change, which Beecher championed, was centered on a new vocation for a gender mostly excluded from other professions.[32] In short, the addition of women teachers transformed the American school. This did not happen all at once. Women's economic opportunities actually contracted after the American Revolution.[33] Yet even during the postrevolutionary backlash, which relegated a women's role in society to being an ideal wife and mother, women were slowly gaining autonomy. The life of Susan Nye Hutchison (1790–1867), of the same generation as Catharine Beecher, Emma Willard, and Mary Lyon, presented a microhistory through Hutchinson's journals. These were firsthand accounts, between 1815 to 1841, of Hutchinson's trek south of the Mason-Dixon Line as a teacher experiencing women's work, social reform, and evangelism. Her experiences also notably included raising a family and making a living. Hutchinson's narratives included recounting incidents such as praying in the streets of Raleigh with slaves and free African Americans and defying North Carolina law by teaching slaves to read.[34]

Yet even as support for the notion of gender equity in terms of similar intellectual ability between men and women was growing, it paradoxically did not include the idea of equal political, social, or economic rights. What socioeconomic gains were made for women and what rights where withheld were due in part to a complex mesh of macro political and economic decisions (e.g., a cash economy necessitated that many people be able to read, write, and do math) that demanded in general a better educated populace that was inclusive of gender but exclusive of race. As attempts were made to respond to societal concerns, the formerly male-dominated status of teaching fell in public regard. In large part this was due to the blatant gender bias of the day as women entered the profession.[35] Matthew Fegan describes a plethora of sociocultural issues, such as the evolving formalization of schools and the culture of benevolence along with traditional gender stereotypes, that formed the teaching profession of the nineteenth century. These detrimental effects have lasted to the present day. The notion of the image of a low social status, low pay, nonintellectual, tightly controlled profession has to a large extent persisted into the twenty-first century, continually threatening the recruitment of new teachers.[36]

A Plan for Inclusion

Even as a layered hierarchy of exclusion was generally (although often cha-
otically), implemented, the forces of inclusion made headway. Slowly and
inexorably public schools became more inclusive even given significant race,
gender, and class restrictions. The broadening of educational opportunities
was observable if uneven. During the first half of the nineteenth century,
although public elementary schools existed in both New England and the
Mid-Atlantic states, the South did not have significant free public education
and the West was still waiting for formal statehood to launch their free public
education plans. Still, the West—subject to a multiplicity of social forces from
the expropriation of land and labor to boomtowns and ghost towns—had a
blueprint to further the cause of public education. The Northwest Ordinance
of 1787 earmarked a plot of land (1 of 36) in every potential township for
the support of education. The measure became a precedent for educational
planning across the nation. The Ordinance proclaimed in Article 3, "Religion,
morality, and knowledge being necessary to good government and the happiness of mankind, schools and the means of education shall forever be encouraged."[37] Jeannie Oakes has written that in 1890 less than one in 10 of the country's teens (between the ages of 14 to 17) attended secondary schools. Yet it
was precisely at this time when seminal events began to take root to increase
the number of students in the classroom. There was tremendous growth of
cities fueled by massive immigration of peoples with different languages and
cultures, the mitigation of child labor, and a strict adherence to compulsory
school attendance. By 1900, 31 states had compulsory school attendance for
students from ages 8 to 14. By 1918, all states required students to complete
elementary school.[38] This new and particular group of pedagogical and social
challenges at the beginning of the twentieth century called out for new ideas
to reform a new entry gate for immigrants—the public school. How America
met these challenges in public schools confirms the aforesaid dual nature of
inclusion and exclusion. That dual paradigm fostered "access *and* advantage,
promoting equality *and* inequality" to produce in the United States a particularly robust educational system, unendingly expanding and yet continually
unequal."[39]

Figure 5. Washington, D.C., schoolchildren (1899?) in a horse-drawn bus.

The Committee of Ten and the Cardinal Principles

In 1892, with the immense growth of secondary education on the horizon, Charles Eliot, then president of Harvard University, chaired the National Education Association's Committee of Ten on Secondary Studies. Secondary schools were mostly an urban institution with few high schools that served the 75 percent of a country that resided in rural areas. Those secondary schools did not at that time serve as a significant bridge to the world of work or to college. In 1893, when the committee submitted their report, only 3.5 percent of students graduated from high school. Notwithstanding the minute graduation rate, the preparation of students for the future via rigorous academic training in classical or modern curricular options was seen at that time as best for all whether students chose to go to college or not. As for higher education, there was a concern. The unsystematic transition between secondary education and college was subjective, with shifting entrance requirements. Significantly, the committee opposed different programs for college-bound

Figure 6. Immigrants in night school (1909) in Boston, Massachusetts.

and non-college-bound students. Their inclusion-minded recommendations indicated a fundamental faith that students from various regions and backgrounds had the intellectual capacity to succeed in secondary and postsecondary studies.

However, Eliot's committee, which forwarded the notion of education for its own sake, appeared to some oblivious to the rapidly changing demographics of massive immigration. While some noted educators of the time, for example G. Stanley Hall, viewed the committee as out of touch with the multifaceted demands that the public schools faced at the dawn of the twentieth century, others strongly disagreed with that notion.[40] As Diane Ravitch noted, the Committee of Ten stood firmly for a liberal education as they were confronted with a hodgepodge due to the idiosyncratic actions by thousands of school boards and colleges. The philosophic center of the 1893 report from the committee was that students should only be limited in school by how far their talents and interests would take them. Moreover, the Committee of Ten stated that all students would benefit by receiving the most enriched liberal education. Indeed, the published report forwarded the egalitarian idea that "every subject which is taught at all in a secondary school should be taught in the same way and to the same extent to every pupil so long as he pursues it, no matter what the probable destination of the pupil may be, or at what point his education is to cease."[41]

Another solution set for the American school was proposed in 1918. A different kind of a high school was about to burgeon. Based on *The Cardinal Principles of Secondary Education*, a report by a special committee of the National Education Association, both academic and nonacademic programs and differentiated curricula were to be established in a single high school. The rationale for the split was to institute the idea of an inclusive high school with a democratic base made up of a cross-section of the community along with the notion of exclusive academic and vocational hierarchies. This in turn was based on the concept of specialization to best serve the needs of a socially efficient industrial America. Here was another example of American dualism in action where separation (between academic and vocational tracks) and subsequent exclusion was to be executed as a "progressive" idea to make the schools more "efficient." Each student—especially the newcomer to U.S. shores whose culture and language was different—was to find and know his or her place in among the new populations in industrial America. Change was manifestly evident in the new kind of student appearing at the classroom door. Over half the students in the 37 largest cities had parents who were born abroad. Lawrence Cremin noted:

> Schools that really wanted to educate these youngsters could not get by with surface changes. The mere fact that children in a single schoolroom spoke [a] half-dozen different languages, none of them English, inevitably altered the life of that schoolroom. And the problem went far beyond language, for each language implied a unique heritage and unique attitudes toward teacher, parents, schoolmates—indeed, toward the school itself.[42]

Apart from the mere crush of numbers of students with new and particular needs, the belief in social stratification as the natural order of things was sustained in the public consciousness. Of course, the ideas of an inherently unequal societal hierarchy had never gone away. In fact, at the end of the nineteenth century the *Plessy v. Ferguson* Supreme Court decision reconfirmed apartheid as a "natural" condition. Throughout the nineteenth and early twentieth centuries separate schools for Native Americans and African Americans were easily observed but under the conventional wisdom and settled law of the day—was seldom questioned. The *Plessy* prec-

Figure 7. African American schoolgirls in a cooking class surround a woodstove (c. 1899).

edent reestablished and strengthened the traditional notion of exclusion that held that "separate" facilities for African Americans and whites were constitutional if they were "equal." Race inferiority was simply the accepted societal view of the time. Correspondingly, as has been noted, women's education was relegated to a few professions (most importantly teaching) that were said to be "fitted by dispositions and habits" to the latter part of the nineteenth century. As for African American future educators—if ever that was to become a possibility—ample caution was advised. The notable essayist, novelist, and editor Charles Dudley Warner suggested, with unwitting condescension, that only a slow, tightly controlled process ("by the white race") was recommended:

> The process of educating teachers of this race, fit to promote its elevation, must be a slow one. Teachers of various industries, such as agriculture and the mechanic arts, will be more readily trained than teachers of the rudi-

ments of learning in the common schools. It is a very grave question whether, with some exceptions, the school and moral training of the race should not be for a considerable time to come in the control of the white race. But it must be kept in mind that instructors cheap in character, attainments, and breeding will do more harm than good. If we give ourselves to this work, we must give of our best.[43]

Still, even given the reentrenchment of white supremacy in law and custom, the nineteenth and twentieth centuries were witness to a classic battle for the soul of American education. Some encounters linked to the movement west by the pioneers were clearly won in the name of a more inclusive and educated society. The ideology of hope and inclusion, opening the way decade by decade to ever greater universal access (by women, people of color, and the new immigrants), can be mapped in America's relentless westward expansion via road, wagon trail, and rail. Students were equipped with *McGuffy Readers*, which sold in excess of 122 million copies, containing stories that pictured children in their relationship with family, teachers, friends, and animals along with moral lessons (e.g., honesty and hard work). The United States now had more children (nearly 13 million in 1890) in public schools than any other country at that time.[44]

A Particular Solution for a Specific Problem

There was a counterpoint to the success of greater inclusion of new immigrants into public education. The massive immigration at the beginning of the twentieth century that numbered Russians, Jews, Italians, and Poles, among others, provided the fuel for anti-immigrant fear and loathing of these new mostly eastern and southern Europeans by the earlier established British and Germanic immigrants who traced their American roots to the eighteenth century. Oakes wrote of this time that "most of the population increasingly feared the potential dangers that could result from what was seen as unrestrained hordes of urban immigrants, and a perception of a need for the exercise of greater social control was widespread."[45] How to meet such a societal challenge? What institution could serve the newcomers? The most widely attended institution was the obvious choice, the last great assembly place of American democracy—the public school. Thus, the public school became systematically geared to meet and manage the particular challenges of the

Figure 8. Columbia, the allegorical female figure of the United States, leading pioneers westward as they journey on foot, in a stagecoach, in a Conestoga wagon, and by rail.

newcomers. The rationale for a systematic approach (e.g., a plan to maintain social stratification by means of a layered hierarchy) to accommodate the new immigrants in the public school classroom had three basic components: justification via Social Darwinism, application of racial superiority via empiricism, and assimilation by means of Americanization.

Social Darwinism as Justification

One of the ideological beliefs that took hold at this time produced a powerful synergy, suggesting a form of cultural and race-based superiority as scientific theory. Much in the tradition of Jefferson's aforementioned "suspicions" based on his notions of natural history in the late eighteenth century, a belief in a form of natural selection was abuzz in the late nineteenth and early twentieth centuries. Ideas of a new society based on science (notably the

Figure 9. Elementary public school students in Washington, D.C. (c. 1899).

appreciation of the concept of survival of the fittest embedded in the theory
of evolution), industry, efficiency, and reform were considered in those days
"progressive" and elemental to the pseudoscientific concept of Social Darwinism. This particular belief system, a product of the nineteenth-century
English philosopher Herbert Spencer, encompassed and for some was seminal in understanding the realms of philosophy, religion, sociology, and pedagogy. Assumptions from the late nineteenth century made about race and
fitness regarding the world of work and education were accepted and even
applauded by members of the American intelligentsia at the beginning of the
twentieth century. Consider the characterization of the African American in
the late nineteenth century. Even slavery could be rationalized in this pseudo-
evolutionary transformation as Warner concluded:

> But slavery brought about one result, and that the most difficult in the devel-
> opment of a race from savagery, and especially a tropical race, a race that has
> always been idle in the luxuriance of a nature that supplied its physical needs

with little labor. It taught the negro to work, it transformed him, by compulsion it is true, into an industrial being, and held him in the habit of industry for several generations. Perhaps only force could do this, for it was a radical transformation. I am glad to see that this result of slavery is recognized by Mr. Booker Washington, the ablest and most clear-sighted leader the negro race has ever had.[46]

White Superiority via Pseudo Empiricism

Accordingly, the notion of survival of the fittest was conveniently transferred from species to races. The "who are we?" question became one of taxonomy and classification interpreted by a race's perceived level of societal development. A rationale for cultural imperialism was thus embedded in the minds of many of the decision-makers who via "scientific testing" (e.g., Louis Terman and Carl Brigham) quantified the superiority of the Anglo-Saxon race. Stated simply, within this "empirical" context the differences among humans could be found in their biology. The dynamic was profound, and in moral terms guilt free—superiority was now considered genetic not social. Implications for prohibiting intermarriage were obvious, lest the race become diluted. The reality of societal evolutionary superiority vs. inferiority (i.e., Anglo Saxons vs. non–Anglo Saxons) in the early twentieth century seemed like a simple case of cause and effect, if one simply looked at the statistical data as it related to poverty, schooling, literacy, and crime when compared to ethnic heritage. The level of expectations for academic development and social growth were charted for each ethnic group by the federal government.

With this "empirical" view in place, an inherently discriminatory brand of pedagogy based on high expectations for some, and the transparent bias of low expectations for others, logically led to a tiered curricular format. Oakes describes how the new secondary schools of the twentieth century differentiated students and implemented curricular levels that had wide social implications:

The comprehensive high school . . . [was] a new secondary school that promised something for everyone, but, and this was important, that did not promise the *same* thing for everyone. Gone was the nineteenth-century notion of the need for common learnings to build a cohesive nation. In its place was curriculum differentiation—tracking and ability grouping—

with markedly different learnings for what were seen as markedly different groups of students.[47]

Tracking was proposed by those who believed in social efficiency. This coincided nicely with the idea of biological race superiority. Such a philosophical belief system promoted a political ideology (Americanism) fostering essentially race-based and gender-based curricular opportunities devised to carry out the mission of generating "productive" citizens for the industrial needs of the nation.

Assimilation via Americanism in the Classroom

To be sustained over a period of time, any new view of such a fundamental notion as *who we are* requires a contemporary supporting political ideology. The practice of grouping students into different tracks had elements of race, gender, and class prejudice stirred into a mixture of empiricism and nationalism. In other words, a political ideology was born from the combination of Social Darwinism (which assumed the natural selection of the fittest) and a new nationalism that was to be sustained via a compliant pedagogy to teach and enforce cultural conformity in the country's public schools.[48] The state-approved vehicle bred from a nationalistic pedagogy was called Americanism. Blended with a mix of patriotic regimentation and a fear of being excluded due to language or culture, a new icon was born—the melting pot. The notion seemed seductively egalitarian—"all for one, one for all," "we are all in the same boat." Notwithstanding, the melting pot became in reality more like a wash tub. Languages (other than English), culture, folkways, and mores other than Anglo-Saxon were to be scrubbed clean from staining the American experience. In essence, assimilation—a form of linguistic and cultural orthodoxy—became an American value. Those who fought against this ideal where somehow considered less American. The progressive mantra of "one nation–one language" during this era was expressed by Theodore Roosevelt: "We have room but for one language here and that is the English language." As for the true meaning of the melting pot, Roosevelt posited, "For we intend to see that the crucible turns out our people as Americans, of American nationality, and not as dwellers of a polyglot boardinghouse."[49] The message was taken to heart by American public schools. Following World War I,

Figure 10. President
Theodore Roosevelt,
1904.

due in part to anti-German sentiment, teaching English as the expression of the official American language was systematically implemented. By 1918, 35 states required that classroom instruction be in English only. During the first decades of the twentieth century, assimilation was more than a politically driven policy—in many jurisdictions, it had the strength of law.

Personification of Duality: Cubberley's Life and Legacy

It was during this era that perhaps the quintessential personification of the uniquely American paradox—a man who moralized over the principles of inclusion while implementing strategies of exclusion—appeared. Such a man was Ellwood Patterson Cubberley (1868–1941). The effects of his legacy (the promotion of empirical research in education and improved efficiency in public schools) endure to this day. Cubberley, whose professional life bridged the nineteenth and twentieth centuries, led a most distinguished career as a teacher, highly influential administrator, and groundbreaking writer in the history of American education. Although after his oral defense of his dissertation at Columbia University, Edward Thorndike commented that Cubberley was "a good man but not a good scholar,"[50] Cubberley's half century of work in the field of education was prodigious. He authored or coauthored nearly 30 books and reports using an evolutionary tone in writing the history of education. He taught a generation of administrators in his "science" of education management, editing nearly a hundred volumes of the then highly regarded Houghton-Mifflin Riverside Textbooks in education (including methodology, sociology, psychology, and administration) that sold over three million copies.

It is difficult to overestimate Cubberly's impact on American education. Cubberley's personal connections helped so many graduates find administrative positions across the nation that his influence was likened to a Tammany Hall boss. Cubberley's professional experience included teaching in a one-room schoolhouse in Indiana, serving as president (1891–96) of Vincennes University, and superintendent of schools (1896–98) in San Diego City Schools. He joined the faculty of Stanford, as an assistant professor of education, and in 1906 rose to the rank of full professor. Significantly, in 1917, he was named dean of the School of Education, a post that he held for over a quarter century until his retirement in 1933. He promoted the field of education as a university study, urging the professionalization of teaching and administration. Cubberley's most important writings include *Changing Conceptions in Education* (1909), *Public Education in the United States* (1919), *The History of Education* (1920), and *Public School Administration* (1929). Noted educational historian David Tyack, writing a biographical sketch in the *Dictionary of American Biography* in 1974, presents Cubberley as the embodiment of the conflict between the hopeful notions of a kind of utopian inclusion for the public school juxtaposed to an American society that openly embraced the inherently excluding dynamic of race and ethnic supremacy.

He praised democracy but sought to remove the control of the schools as far as possible from the people. Although he desired to give teachers professional status, he opposed granting them tenure and a strong voice in educational policies. Urging that education should become "scientific," he nonetheless wrote and spoke with an evangelical rhetoric. Certain ethnic groups he regarded as inherently inferior, yet he believed that education might somehow improve them and save the republic. Skeptical of social reformers and panaceas in other domains, he still maintained a utopian faith in reform through education.[51]

To better comprehend Cubberley's later policies (e.g., grouping by ability or tracking) one must understand his point of reference. His writings reveal his view of world history, pedagogy, and the potential (or lack of it) of students who came to the classroom door. In his 1922 book, *A Brief History of Education*, he viewed American education as standing atop a foundation composed of Greek, Roman, and Christian bedrock, which then was shaped by the Germanic tribes and later sculpted by the Reformation. American history and specifically America's educational heritage in Cubberley's view had specific antecedents that produced a special formula, a superior blend that put the American Republic on an advanced evolutionary track. Therefore, the American experience was destined, if not preordained, to flourish as a democratic culture because it could authentically claim historical and cultural ties with Greece (which was popularly known then as the birthplace of democracy), the Roman Empire, and then via the Germanic tribes to Britain. Cubberley wrote with characteristic certainty that "the first Western nation created from the wreck of the Roman Empire to achieve a measurement of self-government was England."[52]

Thus, from the high culture of Greece represented by Socrates, Plato, and Aristotle, the torch of Western enlightenment is passed to the Romans. The glory of the Roman Empire is celebrated and possessed an intellectual pantheon of scholars and philosophers (e.g., Virgil, Ovid, Cicero, Epictetus, Seneca, Marcus Aurelius, and Boethius). If one needed to preserve an unbroken lineage, a chain of ancestry might be represented by Boethius, a philosopher and Christian martyr who has been called the last of the Romans. After all, the continued existence of Christianity is at least partly attributable to its promotion by the Romans. The final and fourth quarter of influence and the most influential of all were the Germanic tribes, which were viewed as strongly affecting all future "progress and development." Cubberley explained how the German experience during the Reformation (i.e., Martin Luther's contribution) fostered the idea of universal education. Education then became a universal calling. Protestants made a point, according to Cubberley, of individual judgment and individual responsibility. These concepts led Protestants to ideas about the importance of every soul needing an education to better serve their Heavenly Father. Cubberley then goes on to state that from this notion of universal education it was "not a long step" to participation in and responsibility by government. Continuing in that vein, the Protestant Reformation had a significant impact on American education, in Cubberley's opinion, especially given the Calvinistic influence due to its program for "political, economic and social progress. . . . This program demanded the education of all. " Cubberley presented what he believed was a historical lineage that extended back to the ancients. Specifically, it was the Reformation that bred the new settlers, transported via ships to the New World, who carried a certain strain of advanced cultural enlightenment that would so greatly influence the American Republic and its educational system.[53] In short, Cubberley presented a type of royal blood line, a Greek, Roman, Christian and Germanic heritage melded in the crucible of the Reformation, transported from England to take root in pristine American soil.

Cubberley also found it important to state that the American Republic was founded by Protestant Englishmen bringing with them the concepts of constitutional law and participatory democracy:

> Though the early settlement of America . . . was made from among those people and from those lands which had embraced some form of the Protestant faith and represented a number of nationalities and several religious sects, the thirteen colonies, nevertheless, were essentially English in origin, speech, habits, observances, and political and religious conceptions. This is well shown for the white population by the results of the first Federal census, taken in 1790, as given in the adjoining figure. This shows that of all the people in the thirteen original States, 83.5 per cent possessed names indicating pure English origin, and that 91.8 per cent had names which pointed to their having come from the British Isles.

> We thus see that it was from England, the nation which had done most in the development of individual and religious liberty, that the great bulk of the early settlers of America came, and in the New World the English traditions as to constitutional government and liberty under law were early and firmly established. The centuries of struggle for representative government in England at once bore fruit here. Colony charters, charters of rights and liberties, public discussion, legislative assemblies, and liberty under law were from the first made the foundation stones upon which self-government in America was built up.[54]

Note how Cubberley's particular historical perspective joins with the "scientific" view of Social Darwinism. Cubberley is channeling Rudyard Kipling here—an enlightened race (northern European and Protestant) must lead and pick up the "white man's burden" of helping other races that have not reached what then was embodied as the Anglo-Saxon level of development.

> TAKE up the White Man's burden—
>   Send forth the best ye breed—
>   Go bind your sons to exile
>   To serve your captives' need;
>   To wait in heavy harness
>   On fluttered folk and wild –
> Your new-caught sullen peoples,
>   Half devil and half child.[55]

As these Kipling-like ideas merged in Cubberley's writings a conceptual framework grew. It was a mind-set that also descended from the eighteenth-century ideas expressed by Jefferson in his *Notes on the State of Virginia*. The best of humanity, observably the most evolved race, needed to be sent forth to serve the lesser races among us as a parent would help a mischievous child. Such a belief system nurtured organizing principles that became systemic as evidenced in the practices within Cubberley's idea of the "science" of school management. Cubberley's idea of school management was premised on the notion of an educated elite with exclusive decision-making power. He argued strongly against local control as "democracy gone to seed." Rather than actually practice democracy, Cubberley viewed the school as an implement or "instrument of democracy" that needed elite experts in control. An efficient system meant among other things differentiation of the curriculum into separate academic tracks for the students with different ability, which often resulted in differentiated curricula according to race, gender, or class, or a combination of all of these.

Cubberley's Hierarchy

Cubberley viewed Western civilization as preeminent in the world of thought. Consequently, his views of the biological and social inferiority of people of color now under the American flag as a result of the Spanish-American War were predictable. In a chapter entitled "New Tendencies and Expansions" he described a fusion in which the end result was to culturally elevate certain indigenous peoples to the American standard, "where divergent racial types are being fused into a new national unity; in Cuba, Porto Rico, and the Philippines (R. 343) where the United States has used education to bring backward peoples up to a new level of culture, and to develop in them firm foundations of national solidarity."[56] These ideas were not unique to Cubberley. At the very beginning of the twentieth century President William McKinley wrote to the Philippine people that "the mission of the United States is one of benevolent assimilation."[57] The perceived need to counsel America's new colonies gave rise to a more expansive notion of raising cultures around the globe. Once again invoking Kipling's notion of the white man's burden, Cubberley asserts the following in concluding *The History of Education*, which was originally published in 1920:

> In this work of advancing world civilization, the nations which have long been in the forefront of progress must expect to assume important roles. It is their peculiar mission—for long clearly recognized by Great Britain and France in their political relations with inferior and backward peoples; by the United States in its excellent work in Cuba, Porto Rico, and the Philippines; and clearly formulated in the system of "mandatories" under the League of Nations—to help backward peoples to advance, and to assist them in lifting themselves to a higher plane of world civilization. In doing this a very practical type of education must naturally play the leading part, and time, probably much time, will be required to achieve any large results. Disregarding the large need for such service among the leading world nations, the map reproduced on the opposite page reveals how much of such work still remains to be done in the world as a whole. "The White Man's Burden" truly is large, and the larger world tasks of the twentieth century for the more advanced nations will be to help other peoples, in distant and more backward lands, slowly to educate themselves in the difficult art of self-government, gradually establish stable and democratic governments of their own, and in time to take their places among the enlightened and responsible peoples of the earth.[58]

Although Cubberley's words have the distinct ring of the condescension, naiveté, and white supremacy common to the first half of the twentieth century, what is important to note is that he had prestige and power not only as

Figure 11. Uncle Sam as teacher to racially stereotypical new students named "Cuba, Porto Rico, Hawaii, and Philippines."

a respected historian but also as a creator of a new school management style. Significantly, he acted on his beliefs, training a generation of school administrators in what was then known as the "science" of school management.[59] For the first third of the twentieth century Cubberley and his informal network (many of whom, like Cubberley, attended graduate school at Columbia's Teachers College) of superintendents, foundation heads, and other academics forwarded the idea of tracking students. Cubberley's "science" had its genesis in his beliefs about students and their societal status. Cubberley was convinced that having high expectations for students of a lower-class upbringing was unrealistic. His faith in democracy had clear limits that stopped at the border of classism:

> We should give up the exceedingly democratic idea that all are equal and that our society is devoid of classes. The employee tends to remain an employee; the wage earner tends to remain a wage earner. . . . One bright child may be worth more to the National Life than thousands of those of low mentality.[60]

As for ethnicity, Cubberley's prejudice toward race purity, assimilation, and the superiority of the Anglo-Saxon culture was clear when he wrote as early as 1909 in *Changing Conceptions of Education in America*:

> Southern and eastern Europeans have served to dilute tremendously our national stock, and to corrupt our civil life. . . . Everywhere these people tend to settle in groups or settlements, and to set up here their national manners, customs, and observances. Our task is to break up these groups or settlements, to assimilate and amalgamate these people as a part of our American race and to implant in their children . . . the Anglo-Saxon conception of righteousness, law and order, and popular government.[61]

The notion of amalgamation is revealing for it presents the idea of singularity. In other words, the rationale of the melting pot is not to create a mix but to melt all elements into a single body to take form within the Anglo-Saxon mold. The idea of efficiency, born in the experience of the American factory and assembly line, was not lost on Cubberley. In 1916 he wrote of the schools as factories in which

> factories in which the raw materials (students) are to be shaped and fashioned into products to meet the various demands of life. The specifications for manufacturing come from the demands of twentieth century civilization, and it is the business of schools to build its pupils to the specifications laid down.[62]

The "factory" would be controlled by experts with a state-run centralized hierarchy seen as the ideal option. From the platform of a noted Stanford University scholar, Cubberley promoted the notion of professional supervision and control of schools by an administrative elite. The idea of the significance of a classroom teacher or parent as stakeholders was not a consideration. His best-case scenario to "guard the rights and advance the welfare of our children" included a tiered hierarchy of select decision-makers with a type of federal structure led by the national government, a subservient state-level administration, and finally, well down the chain of command, the local school districts.[63]

The factory motif, complete with a top-down organization, answered the problem of the growing number of students from diverse backgrounds via what Cubberley termed the "science of school management." To Cubberley the process of education was a great experiment in social engineering and the public schools were the proving ground to test and confirm this conscious form of social evolution. With efficiency and organization as key values, what was called for was the sorting of students by means of testing and placing those learners into programs by measuring and sorting them per their intelligence quotient—a total score stemming from standardized tests originally believed to evaluate human intelligence. Accordingly, understanding a student's capacity (via an I.Q. test) meant that pupil could be slotted into the proper academic or vocational program. Assembly-line sorting of students could be brought to the schools, yielding social efficiency for the nation. While the school used a management derivation of the factory model, the needs of the nation's economic structure would be met by an efficient educational delivery system. The fundamental plan was considered best suited to meet the needs of students of various intelligence, teaching American civic principles along with moral and economic values, thus yielding both a management and a worker class.

In line with Cubberley's faith in science and idealism was the appointment of Louis Terman to the Stanford faculty. Terman, a psychologist, believed that the I.Q. tests would be transformative in understanding a student's intellectual capacity. Terman had field tested his ideas on nearly two million recruits during World War I. While the average "mental age" of American adults was determined at 13.7 years, significantly, the mental ages of racial and ethnic groups based on these tests were also calculated. The racial and ethnic pecking order, listed from the highest mental age to the lowest mental age, was as follows:

1. England
2. Holland
3. Germany
4. U.S. (White)
5. Canada
6. Norway
7. Ireland
8. Greece
9. Russia
10. Italy
11. Poland
12. U.S. (colored)

Figure 12. Mental aptitude testing, 1943.

The ranking was deemed scientific, and added what was considered at the time to be empirical evidence.[64] Accordingly, the hierarchical layers obviated the need for a process to continually affirm and reaffirm the ethnic rankings, producing a form of societal replication. In 1920, over a million children took I.Q. tests. As for the schools, since intellectual growth after childhood was not considered significant, I.Q. tests acted as pathfinders as to one's appropriate placement in school and ultimately in society. Significantly, after World War I concluded, Carl Brigham, who had worked with Terman and other psychologists on the army mental tests, joined the Princeton faculty. In his influential 1923 book *A Study of American Intelligence*, Brigham concluded that the data from the World War I army mental tests demonstrated the intellectual superiority of what he termed the "Nordic Race." The flip side of his pronouncement pointed directly to the inferiority of what he termed "Eastern Europeans," "Mediterranean peoples," and "Negro races." His findings mirrored the rationale of exclusionary immigration politics in the 1920s. He viewed excluding certain groups of people by a strict immigration policy as a way to control and safeguard what he termed the "American Intelligence." Brigham wrote with great certainty:

> According to all evidence available, then, American intelligence is declining, and will proceed at an accelerating rate as racial admixture becomes more and more extensive. The decline of American intelligence will be more rapid . . . owing to the presence here of the Negro.[65]

Brigham's prominence and influence in American education for the better part of a century cannot be understated. In 1926 he developed the Scholastic Aptitude Test (SAT) for the College Board, affecting the acceptance or rejection of multiple generations of college-bound students to this very day.

The results of these tests would profoundly affect the lives of children. For example, in 1930 over two-thirds of the Mexican American students were rated and grouped apart as slow learners and even mentally retarded by tests administered to kindergartners in Los Angeles. The policy recommendations that emanated from I.Q. rankings seemed to justify categorizing students—just as Cubberley had suggested. Terman believed that test findings and supplementary data (e.g., school accomplishment and personal characteristics) would allow the school to organize students into ability groups. An empirical rationale for a tracking system was confirmed by the educational authorities of that time. The tracks (for higher and lower ability students) based on different I.Q. rankings led to the notion of distinct curricula for different students. Grouping by perceived ability, or what has been termed as "tracking," seemed clearly in line with Cubberley's notion of social efficiency for what he termed the "National Life."

Structured Inequality via Perceived Ability Grouping

Cubberley's mind-set provides insight into the rationale for the practice of perceived ability grouping. His philosophical and professional perspectives were premised on some of the most influential ideas (e.g., Social Darwinism) promoted by intellectuals of the late nineteenth and early twentieth centuries. Social Darwinism is rooted in the writings of Herbert Spencer, Lester Frank Ward, and G. Stanley Hall. Biology, it seemed, was even more important than sociology to the root belief of many Social Darwinists. It has been noted that via the work of Terman and others, educators could now logically postulate that by studying the needs and, with the advent of I.Q testing, the "capabilities" of children, schools could devise different curricula to produce the most socially efficient result. From this neatly flowed a "scientific" plan: the school socialized newcomers via Americanization and steered students into the appropriate educational track to fit the needs of the nation. With its dual or multitrack system (different education for different children), education became a form of empirically based social engineering.

At the turn of the twentieth century Cubberley and Terman saw themselves as within a progressive movement. They believed education was a fundamental means to achieve social progress and reform. In concert with the Jeffersonian eighteenth-century dictum of raking a few geniuses from the rubbish, Cubberley and Terman, both believers in eugenics, defined the rubbish. Through twentieth-century "scientific" testing the students to be discarded in the name of efficiency were effectively children of color and children who did not speak English.

Not all in the progressive movement in education (1880 to 1940) sided with the idea of racial segregation or perceived ability grouping in the name of efficiency. For instance, John Dewey believed in the role of equity, shared experiences, and participation in a democratic society:

> In order to have a large number of values in common, all members of the group must have an equable opportunity to receive and to take from others. There must be a large variety of shared undertakings and experiences. Otherwise, the influences which educate some into masters, [also] educate others into slaves. And the experience of each party loses in meaning, when the free interchange of varying modes of life experience is arrested. A separation into a privileged and subject-class prevents social endosmosis. The evils thereby affecting the superior class are less material and less perceptible, but equally real. Their culture tends to be sterile, to be turned back upon itself; their art becomes a showy display and artificial; their wealth luxurious; their knowledge overspecialized; their manners fastidious rather than humane.[66]

Nevertheless, the rationale and (nearly universal) practice of tracking—a form of structured inequality within a school—remain intact. "The practice of perceived ability grouping, or tracking, is based upon the wide-spread notion that students' intellectual differences are so great that a common curriculum would either slow down the higher-tracked students or hopelessly confuse the lower-tracked students."[67] Notwithstanding the common practice of tracking in twenty-first-century public schools, it has been known for decades that the policy of dividing students into higher and lower curricular tracks does not equalize educational opportunity, increase school efficiency, or meet individual needs. Lower-track compensatory classes do not seem to compensate, and remedial programs have not proven a remedy.[68]

One solution set by those who uphold the idea of inclusion, as opposed to homogeneous tracks, is to simply "detrack" the school and present every student with the most enriched curriculum taught via the widest variety of methodological approaches. The viability of the practice of tracking—its fundamental rationale, tests, and policies—at the beginning of the twentieth century may be viewed today as archaic, insensitive, or biased to those who are now working in the twenty-first-century classroom, yet it still remains a standard way of organizing a student body. In fact, tracking students into groups called the robins or the blue jays, academic or vocational classes, or regular or advanced curriculum continues in most public schools to this very day.

Tracking and Segregation Endure

So, the question must be asked: How then could tracking—a part of the legacy of structured inequality—have lasted into the twenty-first century? David Tyack and Larry Cuban, in a discussion of policy cycles and trends, state that "once established as part of the structure of schooling, innovations might be criticized . . . but rarely abolished." They point to the reality, as Oakes does, that solutions to particular problems are adopted and then become part of the way schools are run long after the perceived problem that triggered the initial "reform" has disappeared.[69] One also needs to consider the tenor of the times at the beginning of the twentieth century. Recall that the perceived problem was the fear and loathing of new immigrants from eastern and southern Europe. To meet the public's anxiety and prejudice, early twentieth-century progressive educators—who Cubberley to a degree represented—met the challenge with a pseudoscientific confidence that bordered on hubris. It was an era of steadfast convictions: science was unbiased and pure, education was a potent antidote to society's ills, and professionalization was the new pathway to have educators make the rules in their field as doctors did with their medical boards and lawyers accomplished through their bar associations. Expertise based on empirical judgment, social concerns, and autonomy was to carry not only the day, but the new century. These forward-looking if naive progressive convictions of that time were all but silent on the issues of civil rights, gender, or disability. This brings us to the school of today in the early twenty-first century, which still proclaims inclusion as it plans for exclusion.

Andrew Highsmith and Ansley Erickson, among others, have constructed from the historical record convincing demographic evidence that racism continues to influence and plainly organizes society via the school to sustain and perpetuate tangible social injustice. Tracking and racism have long been known as two sides of the same coin.[70] Other findings are also instructive. Studies in 2006 indicate that tracking school children into homogenous groups was not based on an accurate assessing of ability, nor did it possess any benefit to learning. Research by Jo Boaler, Marie Curie professor of education at the University of Sussex, which followed 700 teenagers in the United States over four years, demonstrated that children in mixed-ability mathematics classes outperformed those grouped by ability. Confirming research notwithstanding, in the initial decades of the twenty-first century there is no popular political will to integrate or untrack the schools.[71]

Whether by tracking or racial segregation, a system of structured inequality inherently follows a known configuration. It is buttressed by a constancy of traditional exclusion supported by ideas that legitimize and rationalize it (e.g., Social Darwinism, survival of the fittest, which has morphed into so-called free market competition, efficiency, and test scores that rank human beings). The blueprint evident in structured inequality demands the classification, categorization, and ultimately the separating of students. The assumed validity of I.Q. and other standardized tests leads to tacit beliefs about the need to group students by perceived ability into different academic tracks. It has been argued by those who uphold the notion of inclusion that other factors such as inherited wealth, power, and prestige are the actual elements determining an unbroken and enduring legacy of who qualifies for a quality formal education.[72] Racial diversity in the first decade of the twenty-first century continues to grow.

Thus, in terms of the body politic at the beginning of the twenty-first century, the new reality of separate and unequal goes virtually unquestioned. Yet the problem of perceived ability grouping (i.e., tracking) is even more ingrained, yet less visible, in the public school system than typical school-to-school segregation. In fact, the easily identified segregation—*intraschool* tracking (i.e., schools in the same or neighboring school districts that have strikingly different racial populations)—could end tomorrow, and *interschool* tracking (i.e., grouping students within the same school) would still happen.

Interschool tracking into clearly superior and inferior academic groups with its historic socioeconomic and racial divides would still preserve the enduring legacy of exclusion. The *school within a school* model can be a recipe for segregation. Geographical proximity (of diverse students attending the same school) is no guarantor of an equal educational opportunity. True integration does not take place if diverse students are not taking courses in which all members of that diverse population can *learn* together. It is from the shared experience of striving to learn together that the common bonds of respect and friendship are earned.

Those who view inclusion as being an unfulfilled promise hold that public schools practice a form of social stratification that in essence determines *who gets what, how they get it, and why they get it.* Certain individuals and groups are seen to traditionally implement and enforce a homogeneous-elite model (i.e., commonly white as opposed to nonwhite, wealthy as opposed to poor, English speaking as opposed to non-English-speaking students), and therefore the children of the privileged are awarded the best curricular options (e.g., honors and advanced classes). The model is thus regenerated. Significantly, inequality may or may not be accepted by all or even most in the society. Yet it may establish the norm when supported by those with economic interests (e.g., home prices), codified into zoning laws and school district boundaries, and thus becomes an accepted custom that becomes multigenerational. Educational consumers seek markers of distinction for their children, or equal access to those markers.[73]

An underlying argument for exclusion appears to be that excellence in education is more important than racial equality or gender equity. Those who believe in inclusion as imperative perceive that idea as a false dichotomy. They would posit, in general, that in a participatory democracy there can be no excellence in the classroom without equality and equity. Specifically, they would articulate that until tracking and racial segregation is abolished the cavalcade of well-intentioned ideas and programs, from Jefferson's A Bill for the More General Diffusion of Knowledge to President Donald Trump's Furthering Options for Children to Unlock Success, will be continued evidence in terms of racial equality of mighty efforts that produced mighty little. The conflicted American psyche struggles each generation with the key issue that has always been central to the fundamental rationale of the very existence of the American Republic, one of genuine social justice for all people residing in the nation. As long as tracking and racial isolation are the preferred pedagogical options in the public schools, American public education is destined to continue the traditional paradox—matching the impulse of inclusion to the reality of exclusion, yielding an enduring legacy of structured inequality. Part 1 has reflected on the growing phenomena of resegregation in the American education. It has been a saga of conflicted philosophy and practice. We have seen a nation that promoted a public philosophy of inclusion while clearly practicing and in recent years accelerating racial exclusion.

Finally, it is not that Americans do not know how to end segregation or growing resegregation. It is a historic fact that the American public school system went through a period of rapid successful desegregation in the 1960s, even in the Deep South—without a shot being fired. The real question is not whether genuine integration can be accomplished, but how it can happen. For teacher candidates and the public at large, understanding the historical paradox of the American public school, with its archetypal battle between inclusion and exclusion, is the first important step in conceptualizing the injustice done to children who have been historically marginalized. The knowledge of and subsequent rejection of this historic injustice may someday lead to a consensus among the American people that there is no quality education without equality in education. Moving from the paradoxical history of hailing inclusion while practicing exclusion calls for an investigation in part 2 of the political machinations from two political parties that fought over a cycle of segregation, desegregation, and resegregation.

PART 2

The Politics of Structured Inequality from Johnson to Trump

For unless our children begin to learn together, there is little hope that
our people will ever learn to live together.

—THURGOOD MARSHALL

Figure 13. School integration in Washington, D.C. (1955).

The Cycle of Segregation, Desegregation, and Resegregation

The first part of this book outlined the continuing historical paradox found in American schools. Within public education, this last great meeting place of democracy, exists an archetypal battle between inclusion and exclusion played out in the lives of the nation's historically marginalized children. In this struggle the issue of race is primal. Part 1 of the text spanned from the late eighteenth to the early twenty-first century. In those nearly two and a half centuries, America experienced the emergent notion of inclusion via Thomas Jefferson's 1778 proposal to the Virginia Assembly, A Bill for the More General Diffusion of Knowledge. Yet in the twenty-first century America paradoxically considered an argument for extending exclusion in 2016—when the Supreme Court heard arguments that could have effectively ended affirmative action in the American classroom in *Fisher v. Texas*. While the first part of this book focused on a historical overview, this second section will investigate the political roots of resegregation in American public schools and attempt to demonstrate that there has been a preconceived explicit political wedge issue used to wage electoral victories that has produced outcomes that have generated greater racial isolation in America's classrooms. This divisive strategy, made up of white resentment and unadorned racism based in part on eugenics, can be seen in the nineteenth-century pseudoscience labeled Social Darwinism.[1] Significantly, race-based political campaigns, founded in white anger and resentment, were adopted by the segregationist wing of the Democratic Party, then in an ideological flipflop later implemented across the United States beginning in the 1960s by the Republican Party. National elections from the 1954 ruling in *Brown v Board of Education* to the 2016 election of Donald J. Trump indicate the popular appeal of racism and nativism. These tendencies have generally resulted in the body politic's rejection of racially integrated schools and over time predictably accelerated resegregation, providing an ever more separate and unequal American classroom for the nation's youth.

In the era of the Trump administration, over two dozen judicial nominees flatly refused to answer a question at the very center of legal school segregation: Was *Brown v. Board of Education* correctly decided?[2] The politically charged notion of excluding or even deporting historically marginalized people, as in the eighteenth century, was once again being viewed as acceptable and even desirable. In 2019, President Trump, via a tweet, engaged in a trope oft heard in American racist parlance from colonial times to the present day. Trump essentially told four Democratic congresswomen of color to go back where they came from. He wrote that they should "go back and help fix the totally broken and crime infested places from which they came."[3] It was a public display of racist behavior from an American president arguably not seen in over a century. In 1915 Woodrow Wilson stoked public outrage by screening *The Birth of a Nation* at the White House. This D. W. Griffith silent film, originally titled *The Clansman*, told of the heroic actions of the Ku Klux Klan.[4] Such public derogatory remarks or insensitive actions directed at a certain group of people can provide a window into any president's core values on the aforementioned dueling philosophies of inclusion and exclusion. The feelings and thoughts of these two presidents were in all probability based on their authentic beliefs. Concerning these acts and behaviors, neither Wilson nor Trump ever apologized.

Structured Inequality: From Political Strategy to Pedagogical Practice

Following an array of public policies to make education more accessible to racial minorities, the poor, and women (e.g., Head Start, low-cost college loans, the Civil Rights Act of 1964, Elementary and Secondary Education Act of 1965, and Title IX), a social and political backlash rooted in white resentment was spurred on in the 1960s and early 1970s.

Prominent Republican Party leaders, foremost among them Richard Nixon, had witnessed in 1964 that Republican presidential nominee Barry Goldwater had broken through the traditionally Democratic "Solid South" by carrying five states of the old Confederacy. Those states were Alabama, Georgia, Louisiana, Mississippi, and South Carolina. Understanding what explicit issues mobilized southern whites in 1964 led to explicit planning of a Southern Strategy, which just four years later propelled Nixon to the presidency. In 1968, even given the third-party candidacy of George Wallace, Nixon won Florida, North Carolina, South Carolina, Tennessee, and Virginia. This voter realignment shift of southern white voters from the Democrats to the Republicans had generational repercussions. There have been no major national civil rights initiatives on matters of racial equality since the early 1970s.[5] Sub-

Figure 14. Civil rights leaders including Martin Luther King meet with President John F. Kennedy in the Oval Office in 1963 after the March on Washington.

sequent to that breakthrough in the 1960s, nationwide electoral victories by Republicans have directly led to the appointment of conservative judges at all levels of the judiciary and most significantly to the Supreme Court.

Courts and the Persistence of Structured Inequality

The legal history of desegregation, as outlined by Jennifer Ayscue and Erica Frankenberg, covers four basic phases. First, the *Plessy v. Ferguson* decision in 1896 set forth the doctrine of "separate but equal," which gave segregation the strength of law for nearly six decades. Second, in 1947 *Mendez v. Westminster School District of Orange County* found that segregation of Mexican American students in California was unconstitutional. That case encouraged *Brown v. Board of Education of Topeka*. Yet only slight progress to desegregate was made in *Brown v. Board of Education of Topeka* (1954) and *Brown v. Board of Education of Topeka* (1955), which respectively held that separate schools were "inherently unequal" and directed lower courts to order that desegregation proceed "with all deliberate speed." Third, following strong civil rights legislation and a decision by President Lyndon Johnson to fund only integrated schools in the South, steady desegregation occurred from 1968 to 1973. Furthermore, other favorable Supreme Court rulings encouraged desegregation efforts. For instance, *Green v. County School Board of New Kent County* provided guidance on desegregation plans and forbade the use of "choice" plans that provided only limited desegregation. Correspondingly, *Swann v. Charlotte-Mecklenburg Board of Education* approved busing as a tool for desegregation. Moreover, *Keyes v. Denver School District No. 1*, the first case outside the South, held that so-called de facto segregation had affected a substantial part of the school system and therefore was a violation of the equal protection clause, thereby extending desegregation efforts for Latinx students. Nevertheless, during the Nixon administration, starting in the early 1970s, the forces of exclusion reemerged. For example, *Milliken v. Bradley* in 1974 limited interdistrict (from inner city to suburban) remedies to mitigate segregation.

Fourth, there was a clear retrenchment beginning in Ronald Reagan's administration, resulting in the loss of desegregation tools to the present day. In *Board of Education of Oklahoma v. Dowell* in 1991 the Supreme Court held that if the board stopped enforcing its desegregation plan once a district was declared "unitary" it no longer had to maintain desegregation. Likewise in *Freeman v. Pitts* in 1992 school districts were permitted to be released from a court order to desegregate if ongoing racial segregation in a public school district was caused by private rather than state action. Thus, the Supreme Court ruled the federal judiciary has no constitutional authority to order the district to solve the imbalance. Finally, in *Parents Involved in Community Schools v. Seattle School District No. 1* in 2007 the Supreme Court ruled against using the race of an individual student when assigning students to schools.

Even though James Madison's construct of checks and balances relies on an independent judiciary, political winds can be so strong as to tilt the highest court in the land. Whether via election or appointment the men and women who sit as judges emanate from a political process. Although constitutionally the judiciary is a coequal partner along with the executive and legislative branches, nomination and confirmation to the highest rungs of the judiciary are part of an explicit political procedure. Since the landmark decision to integrate public schools in *Brown* in 1954, a movement toward resegregation has been fueled in part by other Supreme Court decisions from conservative justices who were self-described "strict constructionists" or "originalists." That judicial philosophy has had the effect of permitting schools to be more and more racially isolated. It has been noted that resegregation has continued to occur—stealth like—due to the false belief that only private actions rather than governmental policies were driving racially isolated schools.[6] It was in the mid-1970s that the Supreme Court emphasized the importance of local control over the operation of schools in *Milliken v. Bradley* (1974). Significantly, the Court posited that desegregation, "in the sense of dismantling a dual school system," did not necessitate "any particular racial balance in each 'school, grade or classroom." In a 5–4 decision, the Supreme Court held that the district court's remedy (busing students to achieve racial balance) was "wholly impermissible" and not justified by *Brown*.[7]

A human link between *Brown* and *Milliken* is embodied in Thurgood Marshall. In 1954 Marshall, who was an attorney for the NAACP Legal Defense Fund, argued and prevailed in a case for the inclusion of African American students into a formerly segregated school district. Ironically, a generation later he was in the minority as a Supreme Court judge. The 1974 *Milliken* decision (dealing with transporting students between the less affluent inner city of Detroit and the more prosperous suburbs to achieve racial balance) effectively ended busing as a desegregation tool. That result restricted the public schools' use of busing as a tool to bring about integration. In 1974, Marshall stated:

> In the short run, it may seem easier for the court to allow our great metropolitan areas to be divided up into two cities—one white, the other black. But it is a course, I predict, our people will ultimately regret. For unless our children begin to learn together, there is little hope that our people will ever learn to live together.[8]

Scholars such as Ansley Erickson, Andrew Highsmith, and Jonathan Kozol have entered into a research-based discussion on the reality of the resegregation of America's public schools. It is important to conceptualize that segregated communities that lead to segregated schools are not a "natural" phenomenon. The creation and maintenance of racially isolated neighborhoods, and therefore schools, are due to deliberate practices such as racial steering and preferential mortgage underwriting. Public-sector decisions regarding housing, zoning, land use, and transportation have had the effect of subsidizing white suburbanization, affecting who goes to what school. There is a complex mix of individual racism, resistance to desegregation, and historical linkages (among schools, property markets, and labor markets) that reinforce inequality. There is an economic shared calculus that affects school boundary lines and the price of homes. Multiple modes of Jim Crow (i.e., state and local laws to impose racial segregation in the South after Reconstruction that legally lasted until 1965) today do not occur in isolation but are a historical complex web of interactions that include schools, housing patterns, and urban development programs. This mix of private prejudicial practice and public discriminatory policy has become normalized in society and in the classroom.[9]

The Court and "Race Neutral" Diversity

In the summer of 2007, the Supreme Court in 5–4 decisions in *Parents Involved in Community Schools v. Seattle School District No. 1* and *Meredith v. Jefferson County Board of Education*, rejected diversity plans in these two major school districts. Louisville, Kentucky had spent 25 years under a court order to eliminate the effects of state-sponsored segregation. Both districts took race into account in assigning students. Although the Court left the door open for using race in limited circumstances, the decision effectively restricted districts across the nation that strove to attain racial diversity by sending students to selected schools to achieve racial balance. According to Chief Justice John Roberts the districts "failed to show that they considered methods other than explicit racial classifications to achieve their stated goals."[10] Previous to the Supreme Court's rulings, federal appeals courts had upheld both the Louisville and Seattle plans. Some parents affected by the districts' plans disagreed and sued. The Bush administration filed on behalf of those parents. While admitting that racial diversity was a noble goal, it nevertheless insisted that such diversity could be achieved only through what has been termed as "race-neutral means."

In 2015 the Supreme Court heard arguments that would have ended affirmative action in the American classroom and further accelerated growing resegregation. In *Fisher v. Texas*, Chief Justice John Roberts seemed to doubt the concept of race-based affirmative action. Roberts asked when schools could stop considering race and when affirmative action would end. He questioned the value of a diverse classroom as he queried, "What unique perspective does a minority student bring to a physics class?"[11] Cutting to the essence of the exclusionist point of view, made a century earlier by Cubberley, Justice Scalia questioned the academic competence of minority students

at the University of Texas when he posited, "There are those who contend
that it does not benefit African-Americans to get them into the University
of Texas, where they do not do well, as opposed to having them go to a less
advanced school . . . a slower-track school, where they do well."[12] The *Fisher*
case was decided in 2016 after the sudden death of Justice Scalia. Scalia's
death in all probability changed the vote in the *Fisher* case. The then eight-
member Supreme Court ruled 4–3 in the university's favor of an affirmative
action plan that used race as a factor. Justices Anthony Kennedy, Ruth Bader
Ginsburg, Stephen Breyer, and Sonia Sotomayor delivered the opinion of the
Court, with Justices Clarence Thomas, Samuel Alito, and John Roberts dis-
senting. Justice Elena Kagan recused herself from the case. In 2017, President
Donald Trump nominated Neil Gorsuch to the Supreme Court and in 2018
he nominated Brett Kavanaugh. Both were confirmed. Trump had promised
the electorate that he would appoint judges who held Justice Scalia's strict
constructionist (originalist) philosophy. Justices Gorsuch and Kavanaugh,
like Scalia, are considered originalists—those who interpret the Constitution
consistently with the understanding of the intentions of the founding fathers
who drafted and adopted it. This philosophy has proven over time to be a
bedrock of the conservative decision-making process.[13]

Whether a judge sees himself as a strict constructionist or an originalist,
these philosophies are arguably part and parcel of a political ideology that
plays itself out in court decisions. While conservative courts suggest the
notion of race-neutrality (i.e., not to use race as a factor in the determina-
tion of discrimination) to achieve racial diversity, contemporary census data
plainly demonstrates that the schools of the early twenty-first century are
more racially and economically isolated than they have been since the 1960s.
As a consequence, schools are becoming increasingly unequal. Kozol's writings reveal a nation that has simply, unwittingly or not, effectively reaccepted
Plessy's reality of separate but unequal schools. The result is a tangible injustice to the twenty-first century's most vulnerable demographic—poor children. This stands in contrast to those educators who desire a more inclusive
school and society by dispatching racism, sexism, and classism and ending
transparent societal regression. As noted, the election or appointment the
men and women who sit as judges initiates from a political process. Political success rests on effective political strategy. Strategies evolve over time to
enlist the support of voters. One of the most enduring strategies since the
beginning of the Republic is the Southern Strategy.

The Southern Strategy

One categorical political approach that historically continues to divide Americans along the lines of race is known as the Southern Strategy.[14] This politically calculated wedge approach remains a voter appeal plan that has proven efficacious for multiple decades at the national level. For the Republican Party, beginning in the elections of 1972, it has continued to be—with rare exception—an enduring solid block of electoral votes that has lasted to present-day elections. Historically, it was the Democratic Party that during the nineteenth century favored slavery and fought against civil rights reforms to protect its southern voter flank. However, by the middle of the twentieth century Democrats slowly realigned their ideology to embrace civil rights along with the traditional support of organized labor. Accordingly, the Southern Strategy, a one-time staple of the Democratic Party's states' rights (i.e., segregationist) ideology, was adopted, in a historical irony, by the "Party of Lincoln" with the presidential nomination of Barry Goldwater by the Republicans in 1964. Not coincidentally 1964 was the same year as the passage of the Civil Rights Act. Goldwater, the senator from Arizona, had broken with the moderate wing of his Republican Party and voted against that legislation. Although Goldwater did not openly court the racist vote, racists found in Goldwater their vehicle to express white resentment and bigotry. Goldwater had solid support from White Citizens' Councils and the Ku Klux Klan.[15]

Thus began the metamorphosis of the old Confederacy from the Democratic Solid South to the Republican Solid South. This transition played a large role in Republican electoral victories in the presidential elections of 1972, 1980, 1984, 1988, 2000, 2004, and 2016. Correspondingly, by 1994 the same basic strategy was employed by Republicans to consistently win down-ballot races for Congress and statehouses through the early part of the twenty-first century.

In terms of American education, the governing results of the Southern Strategy may be summed up as the use of executive, legislative, and judicial power to halt integration, school district by school district. This occurred via executive policy, legislative acts, and judicial decisions to nullify and lift court orders to integrate schools not only in the South but also across the nation. These actions have produced, since the *Brown* decision in 1954, a record of over six decades of gradual, and now surging, resegregation of the American classroom. Recall that the Democratic Party's original white supremacy–

Figure 15. Ku Klux Klan members support Barry Goldwater's 1964 campaign for the presidential nomination at the Republican National Convention in San Francisco, California.

based strategy lasted from the nineteenth century to 1964. After Reconstruction in the 1870s the Democrats controlled the Solid South, winning virtually all of the electoral votes until the first major cracks in party unity over the question of civil rights in 1948. The immediate result was the rise of the segregationist "Dixiecrats" followed by prominent Southern Democrats later changing their allegiance (e.g., Strom Thurmond, Jesse Helms, and Mills E. Godwin Jr.) to the Republican Party. The long-range effect was that since the mid-1960s the Republican Party's adoption and implementation of a Southern Strategy (i.e., to augment support of white voters by appealing to direct or indirect animus toward African Americans) has played a large part in effectively resegregating public school education.

To be historically accurate, of course, there has always been a segregationist strategy based on the notion of white supremacy since colonial days. Racism has always had a profound and pernicious effect on American institutions from voting to housing to the very opportunity to be educated. The antecedents of the Southern Strategy can be discovered among the many laws that directly affected the lives of those held in bondage before the Revolutionary War. One needs only to read a 1740 South Carolina law, a template for similar eighteenth-century decrees across the South. In "An Act for the Better Ordering and Governing Negroes and Other Slaves in This Province," Section XLV states:

> And whereas, the having of slaves taught to write, or suffering them to be employed in writing, may be attended with great inconveniences; Be it therefore enacted by the authority aforesaid, That all and every person and persons whatsoever, who shall hereinafter teach or cause any slave or slaves to be taught, to write, or shall use or employ any slave as a scribe in any manner of writing whatsoever, hereafter taught to write, every such person and persons, shall, for every such offense, forfeit the sum of one hundred pounds current money.[16]

Slave owners at that time were clearly concerned that a literate slave might be able to forge passes and organize revolts (like the uprising at Stono). The mere act of educating a slave (i.e., then defined in the language of those days as owned Negroes, Indians, mulattoes, and mestizos) in the middle of the eighteenth century was clearly unlawful and carried a stiff monetary penalty (about $13,000 in today's money per offense). Although the prohibition of literacy is an anathema to the notion of an educated democracy, it is important to recall that slaves were considered not just chattel but a potentially dangerous element that needed to be repressed by law and practice. This eighteenth-century mind-set of subjugation of slaves evolved into the nineteenth-century oppression of emancipated former slaves. A repressive and exploitive mentality continued through the twentieth- and twenty-first-century civil rights battles from voting suppression to the denial of fair housing and equal public education. In terms of the public school, the twentieth century records a brief but transient integration of classrooms in the 1960s and 1970s, but then by the 1980s and into the twenty-first century a systematic resegregation of public schools reemerged. The formulation for contemporary school resegregation has provided an enduring legacy of structured inequality. The relationship between the educational practice of separate and unequal schools and political power was then and is now rooted to a great extent in the Southern Strategy.

The Southern Strategy denotes a fundamental appeal that is both racist and regional to garner electoral victories. The term was popularized by Richard Nixon's political strategist Kevin Phillips in 1970. Phillips reasoned that the emerging reality of African Americans voters had value for Republicans, not as potential Republican voters, but instead to frighten "Negro-phobe" southern white voters away from the Democratic Party to a new home in the transformed states' rights Grand Old Party (GOP).[17] Against a background where Jim Crow laws were being overturned by the Civil Rights Act of 1964 and the Voting Rights Act of 1965, the South was ripe for political realignment. This theory of the Solid South's changing political affiliation was evidenced initially by the presidential election of 1964. Although Democrat Lyndon Johnson defeated Barry Goldwater in a landslide vote (61.1 percent to 38.5 percent), Goldwater was the first Republican since Reconstruction to win the states of Alabama, Georgia, Louisiana, Mississippi, and South Carolina. This was a significant and historic political breakthrough. President Johnson, from his days in the Senate, was a keen political power analyst. In promoting and signing civil rights legislation he predicted the southern base of the Democratic Party would suffer. President Barack Obama critiqued Johnson's sociopolitical calculus:

> And he knew that he had a unique capacity as the most powerful white politi-cian from the South, to not merely challenge the convention that had crushed the dreams of so many, but to ultimately dismantle for good the structures of legal segregation. He's the only guy who could do it—and he knew there would be a cost, famously saying the Democratic Party may "have lost the South for a generation.[18]

Although the Civil Rights Act of 1964 was a profound step forward for Amer-ican society, it contained amendments and antibusing provisions that were tailored to keep northern schools free from desegregation. As the bill made its way through Congress, Amendment (401b) to the Civil Rights Act of 1964 actually distinguished between segregation in the South and North. More-over, deleted references to "racial imbalance" in the education section of the bill made the law applicable only to de jure school segregation in the South.

On the political front, after 1964, there now was empirical evidence that white resentment was a factor in Republican electoral preference and could be channeled through the ballot box. Goldwater's breakthrough in the here-tofore Democratic Solid South was based on multiple factors.[19] While it is true that Goldwater took such unorthodox stances as giving NATO com-manders authority to use nuclear weapons, privatizing the Tennessee Valley Authority, and making Social Security voluntary, his allure to voters in the South was that he just one of just six Senate Republicans who voted against the Civil Rights Act of 1964. This 1964 federal mandate explicitly made public racial segregation and discrimination, then legally sanctioned in the states that had made up the old Confederacy, illegal throughout the nation. In the South, the political effect of Goldwater's states' rights stance was stunning. Goldwater won 87 percent of the vote in Mississippi and carried Louisiana, South Carolina, Alabama, and Georgia (he also carried his home state of Arizona). Thus, even though Goldwater polled under 40 percent of the national vote, he began the transformation of the party from its civil rights traditions stemming from Abraham Lincoln to a states' rights party that embraced the southern political traditions that excluded nonwhites from enjoying the same legal rights afforded to whites from public water fountains to public school classrooms. Goldwater's breakthrough in the South did not go unnoticed by Republicans who were otherwise trounced in the 1964 elections. The Johnson landslide, while yielding better than 2–1 Democratic majorities in the House and the Senate, in retrospect was essentially a pyrrhic victory. The potential to build on white resentment, if not white racism, was proven to have electoral potency in the South and eventually north of the Mason-Dixon line for the rest of the twentieth century and into the twenty-first century.

LBJ: Integrate and Get Funding or Stay Segregated and Get Nothing

Given that in 1964 Goldwater's brand of conservatism was repudiated at the polls, it followed that the most politically liberal educational policy of the twentieth century was proposed, passed, and implemented. The most expansive national education bill in the history of the United States was passed in April 1965. President Johnson remarked that the law was designed to "bridge the gap between helplessness and hope for more than five million educationally deprived children."[20] Congress passed the Elementary and Secondary Education Act of 1965, which was an integral component of Johnson's "War on Poverty." By means of a dedicated source of funding (Title I), federal resources were aimed to meet the needs of the poorest, most educationally disadvantaged students. Title I provided a billion dollars to schools with high numbers of children who came from low-income families. Johnson noted that the Congress finally accomplished what it had been trying to do since 1870: to pass a bill to help all American schoolchildren. LBJ clearly saw the money to aid millions of poor children as an investment. He noted that for every one of the billion dollars spent on that program, that outlay would come back tenfold as school dropouts transformed to school graduates. The Elementary and Secondary School Act was itself a political strategy to provide a response to the civil rights demands of the 1950s and 1960s and promote educational legislation as part of an overall plan to fight poverty.

That strategy was a product of three options (two were rejected) that Commissioner of Education Francis Keppel outlined. First, the federal government could provide general aid to public schools. Keppel felt this might elicit a negative reaction from Catholic schools. Second, the federal government could deliver aid to both public and private schools; here, Keppel noted constitutional obstacles and the possibility of negative reaction from the National Education Association on public funds going to private schools. Third, Keppel's memo forwarded the notion that was eventually adopted—to garner the support of most by making the focus of the law educational aid to poor children.[21] Significantly, the Elementary and Secondary School Act set a paradigm for later public educational policy—categorical aid tied to national educational law. Questions regarding aid to religious schools were not confronted directly because state departments of education administered the federal funds to benefit the child, not the private, parochial, or public schools. Amended in both 1965 and 1968 (to add Title VII, the Bilingual Education Act) the Elementary and Secondary Education Act paved the way for Title IX in 1972 (prohibiting discrimination on the basis of sex in any federally funded education program), thus converting a liberal political agenda into a national education policy.

Johnson believed, perhaps to some extent based on his experience as a public school teacher of Latinx school children in 1928, that society would pay a higher price for poverty and prejudice if it did not invest in the futures of the young.[22] Johnson's initiatives from Head Start (federal support to provide early childhood education, nutrition health, and parent involvement services for low-income children) to low-cost college loans to the spending of $4 billion to help students previously marginalized by grinding poverty, were extraordinary for their time. Significantly, Johnson did not simply articulate a politicians' platitudes about equal opportunity for all; he clearly intended to end segregation. His political plan was created within the reality that most school systems had simply ignored: the genuine integration of schools "with all deliberate speed" as ordered by the 1954 *Brown* decision.[23] The potency of Johnson's policy and practice emanated from the decision to attach strings to federal funds. School districts were given a choice: integrate and get funding, or stay segregated and get nothing.

The change was sweeping and virtually occurred without violence. Accordingly, an apartheid South was transformed with amazing speed—91 percent of southern black children attended integrated schools by 1972. During the middle 1960s and 1970s American public school classrooms in the South (the 11 states that made up the old Confederacy) became the most integrated schools in the United States.[24] While the Johnson presidency may have stirred white resentment founded on racial animus for some, if demonstrations and congressional hearings are a measure of discontent, a greater and more divisive issue at that time was the war in Vietnam. As much as any other factor it was the conflict in Southeast Asia that ended rapid school integration—as Johnson refused to run for reelection in 1968. With his retreat from the political battlefield, the integrated classroom had lost its champion.

Political Ambiguity on Integration

The year 1968 witnessed not only the assassinations of Martin Luther King Jr. and Robert Kennedy and numerous race riots, but it also experienced a tumulus national party convention where a divided Democratic Party nominated Hubert Humphrey. Humphrey was historically supportive of civil rights. Twenty years earlier, at the Democratic Convention in 1948, Humphrey gave strong vocal support to the party's civil rights plank to urge his party to "get out of the shadow of states' rights and walk forthrightly into the bright sunshine of human rights."[25] Nevertheless, Humphrey's record on school integration was, like that of nearly every politician at the time, complicated. Even as a leading sponsor of the Civil Rights Act of 1964 he wrote two amendments to outlaw busing. Humphrey said at the time that "if the bill were to compel it [forced busing], it would be a violation [of the Constitution], because it would be handling the matter on the basis of race and we would be transporting children because of race."[26] One of the few Democrats at the time to stand for busing as a tool to integrate public schools was South Dakota senator and future Democratic presidential nominee George McGovern. Vice President Humphrey's Republican opponent in the general election was former vice president Richard Nixon. Nixon had lost to Kennedy in 1960 and then to Pat Brown in the California gubernatorial race in 1962, which seemed at the

Figure 16. President Nixon, in Washington (1969), throwing out the opening game ball in what was then America's pastime.

time to write his political epitaph. However, unlike his earlier races, Nixon in 1968 more fully understood the potential of using the Southern Strategy as an approach. He became adept at using a race-based appeal to white voters so as to intentionally convert white resentment to recent federal civil rights laws into a powerful voting constituency. Nixon, although publicly not labeled as a bigot in the 1960s, harbored—as did some of his white supporters—racist attitudes toward African Americans, referring to them repeatedly in private (evidenced via taped conversations) as "jigs," "jigaboos," and "niggers."[27]

Of course, the notion of a Southern Strategy was always based on the foundation of white supremacy, which found its home in conservative thought in the 1950s. For example, in 1957 the conservative magazine *National Review*, founded by the most revered and authoritative conservative of the twentieth century, William F. Buckley, intoned in an unsigned editorial that the South "must prevail." Buckley asked whether the white community was "entitled to take such measures as are necessary to prevail, politically and culturally, in areas in which it does not predominate numerically?" He answered, "The sobering answer is Yes—the White community is so entitled because for the time being, it is the advanced race." In a 1960 editorial, the *National Review* concluded, "In the Deep South the Negroes are, by comparison with the whites, retarded."[28] Although in later years Buckley recanted his position and supported federal intervention to protect civil rights, his publication helped unleash racist thought as an electoral element to the political landscape in the late fifties and early sixties. As a precursor to success at the ballot box, in the February 12, 1963, issue of *National Review*, the magazine's publisher, William Rusher, gave a geopolitical prescription for the 1964 election. In short, he recommended that Goldwater appeal to disaffected whites in the South as a pathway to victory.[29] Four years later, as has been noted, it was Nixon who would adopt and refine the Southern Strategy during the presidential campaign of 1968.

Nixon's Rise Bolstered by the Southern Strategy

In terms of the Southern Strategy history records the electoral efficacy of this approach explicitly aimed to appeal to white resentment under the banner of states' rights. States' rights, local control, or an anti-Washington message was a consistent theme on which Nixon in part won the presidential election in 1968. Correspondingly, Nixon ran on a campaign that promised to restore "law and order." Of course, the restoration of law and order would not be done federally as Eisenhower had done with the National Guard in Little Rock, Arkansas, in 1957 to integrate Central High School. In the Jim Crow South, the notion of "support your local police"—in the context of the times—was meant in part to counteract any federal intervention to protect civil rights, which included efforts to desegregate the schools. The Southern Strategy worked on two state-by-state fronts—for Nixon's Republican Party

Figure 17. Alabama governor George Wallace in a doorway at the University of
Alabama in 1963 attempting to stop integration.

and George Wallace's American Independent Party. Former Democrat and
Alabama governor Wallace, who authored the phrase "segregation now, segregation tomorrow, segregation forever," received 13.5 percent of the vote
nationally, but much more significantly won five states and their 46 electoral
votes (Alabama, Arkansas, Georgia, Louisiana, and Mississippi).

However, Nixon won Florida, North Carolina, South Carolina, Tennessee, and Virginia, while Democratic nominee Hubert Humphrey won a single southern state—Texas. By being an unabashed supporter of segregation,
Wallace (like Goldwater did four years earlier) broke through nearly a century
of Democratic Party control in the Solid South, which ultimately worked in
Nixon's favor against Humphrey in the electoral college. Even with a split
vote in the South, this was a watershed moment. The political beneficiaries
of racially charged electoral politics, inherent in the Southern Strategy and
based fundamentally in white resentment, had shifted from the Democratic
Party to the Republican Party. To this day that swing continues to have an
effect on national voting results.

Nixon's Ambiguity on Integration and the Courts

In 1968, even as schools were becoming more integrated in the South, for which President Johnson had risked political capital, northern cities were engaged contemporaneously in school and neighborhood discriminatory practices. One remedy to integrate schools in the north was busing students within the city limits. In 1971, the Supreme Court in *Swann v. Charlotte-Mecklenburg Board of Education* found that federal courts had the discretion to include busing as a desegregation tool to achieve racial balance.

By 1972, after a federal judge ordered that students be bused from the city to the suburbs and vice versa, 800,000 students were affected. That decision, as has been noted earlier in part 2, was appealed in *Milliken v Bradley*. The 1972 prointegration judgment was overturned in the 1974 *Milliken* decision. That 1974 ruling pointed out the distinction between de jure (by law) and so-called de facto (by fact) segregation. In *Milliken* the Supreme Court stated that segregation was allowed if such segregation was not the explicit policy of each school district. Correspondingly, as long as it could not be demonstrated that school systems had each deliberately engaged in a policy of segregation, the school systems were not responsible for desegregation across district lines. President Nixon held a nuanced public position similar to that of the Supreme Court.

Nixon's policies had political roots. Nixon felt in the 1968 presidential campaign that "school desegregation emerged as the administration's most important and enduring (anti) civil rights crusade."[30] In 1970, Nixon eventually supported busing for de jure desegregation in the South but opposed it everywhere else when it was termed de facto segregation.[31] Nixon's calculated stance was based on the notion that the nation's chief executive had to uphold settled law. Once the Supreme Court had decided *Brown*, Nixon as chief executive had to execute the law, stating, "Where it has spoken, its decrees are the law."[32] On the other hand, with the rise of white flight and private academies then taking the place of public schools, Nixon's (and most politicians of whatever stripe) failure to take a stand against racism, regardless of whether it was termed de jure or called de facto, kept his adopted Southern Strategy in play—not only in the South, but with all who feared integration. To many historians, Nixon was a polarizing force who despite court rulings attempted to delay or end school desegregation. "Nixon had to be hauled kicking and screaming into desegregation on a meaningful scale, and he did what he did not because it was right but because he had no choice."[33]

The effect on public schools took the country from a brief epoch of prog-

Figure 18. Children on a school bus riding from the suburbs to an inner-city school, Charlotte, North Carolina in 1973.

ress in classroom integration to decades of increasing racial isolation via an explicit political calculation. In short, Nixon acted to "withdraw the federal government from its efforts at desegregation."[34] The carefully crafted Nixonian polices to permit racial isolation in schools by opposing busing ran counter to the attempts to integrate white neighborhoods (a major cause of racially isolated schools) by his own secretary of Housing and Urban Development, George Romney. This conflict in social and political policy due to Nixon's lack of support of neighborhood integration caused Romney's resignation.[35] Even before the Romney resignation in 1973, another member of the administration left Nixon's team for taking a principled stand about school desegregation. Leon Panetta, Nixon's 30-year-old director of the Office of Civil Rights, wanted to commence desegregation in many southern school districts but found himself caught between the law and the Southern Strategy. Panetta recalled, "I had just been fired from a $30,000-a-year Government job for taking that job too seriously."[36] Unlike the resignation of George Romney, who returned to private life, Panetta forged a political career that has lasted a half century. Elected to the House of Representatives from California in 1976, Panetta served in Congress until 1993, when he was named as the director of the Office of Management and Budget (1993–94), and later in that year as chief of staff (1994–97) for President Clinton. He then served President Obama as director of the Central Intelligence Agency (2009–11) and as secretary of defense (2011–13).

Principled resignations can have the effect of bringing moral clarity to an issue. Panetta's stated reason for leaving the Nixon administration in 1970 was to point to the injustice of segregation in America's schools and his disapproval of Nixon's "deliberate gradualism" façade. Other politicians, from every political stripe in the 1970s, were opposed to or vacillated on the question of school integration (e.g., many well-known Democrats did not support busing as a tool to desegregate schools, including Hubert Humphrey, Joe Biden, and Jimmy Carter). Panetta, however, brought lucidity to the issue when he stated, "The issue is a fair break in education for the kids who have lost out time and again because of rank discrimination. The issue is the future of this nation's race relations, and no amount of escape from the reality will change those issues for us."[37] The relationship between segregated neighborhoods and segregated schools demonstrated an obvious link to the racial isolation that Nixon decided not to address via neighborhood integration or the tool of school busing to achieve racial balance.

Of course, this was part of Nixon's Southern Strategy as evidenced by White House chief of staff H. R. Haldeman's notes of a promise that Nixon made to Southern Republicans. Specifically, Nixon would back off on civil rights and "lay off pro-Negro crap" once he was president.[38] Nixon's antibusing rhetoric affected the entire political landscape. As has been noted earlier, even historic pioneers of racial integration like former vice president and Democratic senator Hubert H. Humphrey of Minnesota were apt to side with Nixon. Humphrey stated that Nixon's policy represented some of "the things that some of the rest of us have been trying to do" Later Humphrey said—arguably disingenuously—that he had not read the fine print of Nixon's policy. However, the liberal senator remained in the camp of those who stated throughout the 1968 presidential primaries that if elected he would limit busing.[39] As a result of Nixon's political maneuver, his popularity among those who opposed either neighborhood or school integration rose. The political scheme paid off in the 1968 presidential race and even more in the 1972 presidential election where Nixon garnered more than 70 percent of the popular vote in most of the Deep South (Alabama, Georgia, Florida, Mississippi, and

South Carolina). To put it in stark terms, of those states that legally mandated apartheid public schools until 1954, Nixon won more than 65 percent of the votes in the states of the former Confederacy. The electoral realignment of the Solid South via the Southern Strategy was now complete. Significantly, Nixon carried 61 percent of the popular vote nationally, which appeared to be clear evidence that white resentment was not confined to the South. In an electoral sense the Southern Strategy was gaining a national appeal. Nixonian policies, which effectively rolled back school integration, were so well established that they continued even after his 1974 resignation to avoid what was considered certain impeachment due to the Watergate scandal.

Ford Continues Nixonian States' Rights Policies

Upon taking the oath of office in 1974, President Gerald Ford continued the same anti-integration policies in neighborhoods and public schools as Nixon. Ford's signature to an antibusing bill was typical of his intention to roll back the efforts to integrate the American classroom. In March 1974, the House of Representatives, by a vote of 293 to 117, passed an antibusing addition to H.R. 69, the Education Amendments of 1974. The amendment "prohibited federal courts or agencies from ordering busing of students to any but the school closest or next closest to the student's home." Later a conference report on the bill adopted the Senate amendment prohibiting busing "beyond the school next closest" to a student's home but allowing courts to mandate additional busing "if it were required to guarantee the student's civil rights."[40] In accordance with Nixon's political rationale, Ford wanted to restrict court-ordered busing aimed to desegregate many large and midsized urban areas: "Busing is simply a remedy to achieve a correction of an alleged act by a school board to violate somebody else's constitutional rights. Busing itself is not a constitutional right, nor is it a lack of a constitutional right. It is only a remedy." Similar to many politicians in the 1970s Ford's views on race seemed conflicted. While supporting the *Brown* decision, Ford was firmly against busing, as it was unpopular and against his conservative values. As president, he philosophically opposed federal intervention to promote integrated schools.[41] After a tough primary battle with Ronald Reagan, Ford left the Republican convention behind 34 points in the polls to Democratic nominee Jimmy Carter. Ford was never able to diversify his political base.[42]

Figure 19. President Gerald Ford with George Wallace at a campaign stop in the South in 1976.

Jimmy Carter, a Son of the South, Disrupts the Southern Strategy

Pitted against a popular governor from the South, James Earl (Jimmy) Carter, the Ford campaign in 1976 failed to execute a completely successful Southern Strategy. In a sense, white regionalism trumped white resentment. Nonetheless, the 1976 presidential election was the last time that Alabama, Mississippi, South Carolina, and Texas would vote for the Democratic candidate for the next 10 presidential elections including the election of 2016. Significantly, Carter was for a time seen as a leader from the "New South" emerging after a turbulent era that included the Vietnam War, the Watergate scandal, and the Nixon pardon. Like Ford, Carter was conflicted when it came to school integration policy, especially previously racially homogenous communities.[43] As governor of Georgia Carter was a proponent of civil rights. For instance, he increased the number of African America state employees, state board members, and judges, and ordered that portraits of Martin Luther King Jr. be hung in the Capitol Building. Yet as enlightened as these actions appeared, when it came to integration of public schools, Carter cosponsored an anti-busing resolution with segregationist George Wallace at the 1971 National Governors' Conference. Five years later, as a presidential candidate in 1976, Carter stated: "I am not going to use the federal government's authority deliberately to circumvent the natural inclination of people to live in ethnically homogeneous neighborhoods. I think it is good to maintain the homogeneity of neighborhoods if they've been established that way."[44]

In addition, during the Carter presidency, congressional roadblocks to desegregation were also put in the way of his administration. In 1977 the Department of Health, Education and Welfare was no longer able to require school systems to bus students to achieve school desegregation. The reason was the passage of the Eagleton-Biden amendment, which prohibited the use of federal funds to require busing, which foreclosed a fundamental tool for desegregating schools. On the other hand, Carter understood that the surging growth of Christian private academies was an attempt to circumvent court-ordered school integration in the South. In 1978, the Internal Revenue Service announced it planned to revoke the tax exemption of schools known as Christian "academies."[45] The conflicted policies of both Ford and Carter were soon to give way to those who openly opposed policies to further integrate the American classroom as resegregation in the 1980s was about to accelerate.

Reagan Nullifies LBJ's Integration Legacy via the Southern Strategy

Ronald Reagan was elected president in 1980. In many ways, Reagan's rejection of using the federal government to promote school integration upended Johnson's hopes, over time, of integrating classrooms across the nation. Reagan's federal policies of pushing back on desegregation can be viewed through the prism of how he campaigned for the presidency. Reagan made a conscious effort from his initial campaign itinerary to emphasize the Southern Strategy pathway to the presidency that Goldwater pioneered and Nixon had followed. Reagan chose a place at a time where the symbolism of what he stood for could not be mistaken by southern white voters. The very first stop of his campaign for the presidency was at the Neshoba County Fair, only seven miles from Philadelphia, Mississippi—best known in history as the place where three civil rights workers, James Earl Chaney of Meridian,

Figure 20. Jimmy Carter and Senator Hubert Humphrey at the Democratic National Convention, New York City in 1976.

Mississippi, and Andrew Goodman and Michael "Mickey" Schwerner of New York City, were murdered. These three slain civil rights workers had been in Mississippi to register African American voters in 1964. Reagan took the stage at the fair and proclaimed his belief in states' rights. States' rights to many was code. Its meaning ranged from a sharp disagreement, especially in the area of civil rights with federal law, to the notion of nullification of federal law. Many who supported states' rights did so in the mid to latter part of the twentieth century to oppose the idea of equal treatment under the law for nonwhites, especially in terms of voting rights and school integration. Race-baiting in order to capture the white vote had become a tradition in the South among conservative politicians.

Later, as president, when it came to the integration of public schools, Reagan governed as a states' rights advocate across a range of social issues. Earlier as a supporter and surrogate for Barry Goldwater, Reagan opposed the landmark Civil Rights Act of 1964. As president, he was open in his opposition to a national holiday for Martin Luther King Jr. and vetoed sanctions on the apartheid government of South Africa (his veto was subsequently overridden by Congress). Although never making openly racist remarks in public, Reagan's description of African delegates to the United Nations in a private (taped) conversation with president Nixon was revealing. In 1971 the UN

Figure 21. President Ronald Reagan in the Oval Office, photo taken between 1981 to 1986.

voted to seat delegates from the People's Republic of China rather than from Taiwan. This prompted the pro-Beijing Tanzanian delegates to break out in a victory dance. The day following the vote, an exasperated Reagan complained to Nixon, "To see those, those monkeys from those African countries—damn them, they're still uncomfortable wearing shoes!"[46]

Reagan Reverses Policies against Race Discrimination

In terms of specific education policy Reagan tried and succeeded in eliminating the federal ban on tax exemptions to private schools that practiced racial discrimination. In the 1983 case of *Bob Jones University v. United States*, the Supreme Court noted the compelling government public policy of eradicating racial discrimination and therefore held that the religion clauses of the First Amendment did not prohibit the Internal Revenue Service from revoking the tax-exempt status of a religious university. At that time Bob Jones University prohibited "admission to applicants engaged in an interracial marriage or known to advocate interracial marriage or dating." Furthermore, Bob Jones University imposed a disciplinary rule that banned interracial dating. Even though the Supreme Court voted 8–1 to allow the IRS to reject the university's tax-exempt status, the decision was controversial. Significantly, Justice William H. Rehnquist was the lone dissenter, arguing that Bob Jones University's charitable status made it tax exempt.[47] Over time, this single minority opinion became—with the support of Ronald Reagan in school discrimination cases—a dispositive factor to halt desegregation and spur resegregation. Just three years later, in 1986, Rehnquist, a 1971 Nixon appointee to the highest court, was appointed by Ronald Reagan to be the sixteenth chief justice of the Supreme Court. Rehnquist had long been the Court's most conservative member.[48] He served from 1986 until his death in 2005. Pointedly, in January 1982—before the Supreme Court decision to revoke tax-exempt status for Bob Jones University—the Reagan administration's Department of the Treasury, with the advice of the Department of Justice, reversed its interpretation of the law. The Treasury Department stated that it would no longer revoke or deny tax-exempt status for religious, charitable, educational, or scientific organizations on the grounds of their nonconformity with fundamental policies. This included the national policy against racial discrimination. Reagan's hands-off policy in terms of federal action extended from private schools to public schools. In a speech in 1983, Reagan stated his opposition to federal intervention into public schools, even to end injustices:

> About 20 years ago, Congress passed the first large-scale aid to public schools. . . . As some of us had warned, with federal aid came federal control. . . . Over the same period, the schools were charged by the federal courts with leading in the correction of long-standing injustices in our society: racial segregation, sex discrimination, lack of opportunities for the handicapped. Perhaps there was simply too much to do in too little time, even for the most dedicated teachers and administrators. But there is no question that somewhere along the line many schools lost sight of their main purpose. Giving our students the quality teaching they need and deserve took a back seat to other objectives.[49]

Reagan framed the debate about public education in terms that made fighting injustice an opponent of quality education. In the 1980s public schools were educating the greatest proportion of the population in schools in the nation's

history. Almost the total school age population was enrolled. The American
public schools were at that time the most integrated in the history of the
nation. Reagan's conservative argument was that quality standards were slip-
ping. The conservative solution, in line with the Southern Strategy, was in
part to dismantle piece by piece government actions to integrate the public
schools.

Reagan: Busing to Desegregate—Waste of Time and Public Money

Accordingly, when President Reagan took office in 1981 federal financial support for desegregation was eliminated. William Bradford Reynolds, the head
of the Justice Department's Civil Rights Division, stated that his department
would not "compel children who do not want to choose to have an integrated
education to have one."[50] Within the social and political context of Reagan's
lifetime, his stances were quite orthodox from a conservative point of view.
As previously mentioned, he opposed the Civil Rights Act of 1964. Likewise,
he opposed the Voting Right Act of 1965, noting that the law was "humil-
iating to the South."[51] Ronald Reagan opposed busing, calling it a waste of
time and public money that could undermine the quality of public schools.
Indeed, Reagan had consistently opposed school busing to integrate schools
long before becoming the nation's chief executive.[52]

After the Civil Rights Act of 1964 was passed, if schools did not desegregate, federal aid would be curtailed. Moreover, swift action by the Justice
Department would follow—and Justice never lost a case. As has been noted,
it was under Reagan's Justice Department that court orders promoting school
integration were aggressively reversed. This 1980s trend and the practice of
ignoring the enforcement of integration efforts has lasted well into the second decade of the twenty-first century.

Historically, Reagan's opposition to Johnson's integration policies were a
stunning about-face. In the 1960s quantifiable progress in the racial integration of the American public school was a political and pedagogical reality.
Recall that in 1963, only 1 percent of black children in the South attended
school with white children. But only at decade later the South had been transformed. In fact, 90 percent of black children attended desegregated schools
in the early 1970s.[53] Many times, this happened via court orders in the South.
Johnson's achievements in civil rights via the legislative and judicial branches
were also used to end what was termed de facto segregation in schools in

other parts of the nation. However, under Reagan during the 1980s there was virtually a complete turnaround of policy that extended from the Department of Justice to the Department of Education. Reagan's actions proved to be the antithesis of Johnson's plan to integrate the American classroom. More than any other president, Reagan's policies are most responsible for the resegregation of the American public school.

George Herbert Walker Bush and an Evolving Southern Strategy

In the election of 1988, Reagan's vice president became the forty-first president of the United States. George Herbert Walker Bush served one term from 1989 to 1993. One of the chief political strategists of that era was Lee Atwater. He had been adviser to President Ronald Reagan, campaign manager for President George Herbert Walker Bush, and became chairman of the Republican National Committee. Atwater, from South Carolina, understood and practiced the Southern Strategy based in part on the work of Harry Dent Sr., who in the 1950s joined Senator Strom Thurmond of South Carolina. Thurmond ran for president as a segregationist Dixiecrat in 1948. It was fellow South Carolinian Dent who early on helped articulate the Southern Strategy using a "law and order" theme. Atwater understood that the Southern Strategy was based on white resentment and historic notions of white supremacy. Over time such a Southern Strategy via various code words could morph into a more respectable political discourse while bringing out the same racist voters to the polls. Atwater explained that the Southern Strategy, with a foundation of blatant racism, was key to winning the Solid South.[54] Although Atwater stated that Reagan did not need a Southern Strategy, Atwater attested to the implicit racism of Republican campaigns. Such divisive strategies have been noted by many scholars. Daryl Michael Scott pointed to racial conservatives who, promoting white contempt for blacks, used various tropes of stereotypical innate inferiority to justify exclusionary policies.[55] Atwater noted that voters did not need to hear explicit race divisive speeches, because the notions of fiscal conservatism, balancing the budget, lowering taxes, law and order, and cutting services like food stamps acted as a code:

> You start out in 1954 by saying, "Nigger, nigger, nigger." By 1968 you can't say "nigger"—that hurts you. Backfires. So you say stuff like forced busing, states' rights and all that stuff. You're getting so abstract now you're talking about

Figure 22. Senators Bob Dole and Chris Dodd bookend "Speech Report Card" with an A+ for President George H. W. Bush.

cutting taxes, and all these things you're talking about are totally economic things and a byproduct of them is blacks get hurt worse than whites. And subconsciously maybe that is part of it. I'm not saying that. But I'm saying that if it is getting that abstract, and that coded, that we are doing away with the racial problem one way or the other. You follow me—because obviously sitting around saying, "We want to cut this," is much more abstract than even the busing thing, and a hell of a lot more abstract than "Nigger, nigger."[56]

The policies under George Herbert Walker Bush in terms of the sudden and then sustained halt to federal support of integration in the public schools mirrored the Reagan plan—and pleased those who fought integrated schools. Even given various reforms, as with learning standards initiatives or school finance redistribution claims via state courts, schools were becoming more unequal. Such reforms could be viewed as ultimately counterproductive since they seemed to tacitly accept the return of school segregation. During the Bush administration, the federal courts all but lifted school desegregation orders. Many urban districts were permitted to return to "neighborhood schools" or "freedom-of-choice" plans, which tended to result in ever more racially imbalanced enrollments. Recall that the aforementioned 1974 deci-

Figure 23. Senator Strom Thurmond in 1961.

sion in *Milliken* reduced desegregation to the boundaries of a municipality. During the Bush years (1989–93), as a consequence, resegregation began to grow as urban schools filled with greater and greater concentrations of minorities, thus increasing racial isolation. Significantly, it was under President George H. W. Bush, in the 1990 case *Oklahoma City v. Dowell*, that for the first time Bush's Department of Justice argued against mandatory school desegregation before the Supreme Court. The Court agreed with the Bush administration.[57] One by one during the 1990s federal courts released schools from busing plans. Efforts to improve the academic development of students were aimed within schools that were becoming more and more segregated. The Bush agenda implicitly and silently accepted that African American and Latinx students would become more and more racially isolated. Given the Supreme Court rulings, the legacy of the Reagan years, and the dropping of court orders to integrate, the outcome was not only the acceptance of what was called de facto segregation but a signal that a new variety of de jure segregation was a tolerable way to resegregate the American classroom.

Southern Ticket of Clinton and Gore Win as Resegregation Persists

The first Democrat to inhabit the office of the presidency since Jimmy Carter was another son of the South, William Jefferson Clinton. Bill Clinton had beaten the Southern Strategy by winning a plurality in the popular vote, which in a three-candidate election (George W. Bush, Clinton, and Ross Perrot) allowed Clinton a large electoral college margin. The former governor of Arkansas doubled down on appealing to a southern constituency by selecting another southerner, Al Gore, a senator from Tennessee, to be his running mate in the 1992 race. In both the 1992 and 1996 elections Clinton and Gore were able to create significant electoral openings in the heretofore Republican Solid South. However, electoral victory to win the White House is one thing—the Southern Strategy had been played since 1964 and left more than a residue of conservatism. There was a cadre of Republican officeholders and judges—and their elections and appointments for nearly three decades had consequences. Even as Clinton in 1992 personally carried a hope for a new era of progressive civil rights policies, the political reality created by the Southern Strategy based on white privilege and white resentment stopped any effort in that direction by the Clinton administration. The political environment that allowed both societal and school segregation was enabled via a variety of factors. There were conservative appointments to the federal bench, conservative legislators at the state and national level, and a growing climate of tacit acceptance of racial isolation in American society in general and the public school classroom in particular. Clinton's pledge to choose a cabinet that "looked like America" gave hope to civil rights advocates. However, the Clinton administration's policy in regard to public school integration reflected the ambiguity of Jimmy Carter's policies 20 years earlier. On the fortieth anniversary of *Brown*, President Clinton praised school desegregation without a single mention of court-ordered busing. In fact, the word "busing" and the term "school desegregation" were nonexistent in all accounts of the president's speeches.[58] Clinton's avoidance of this issue was a political acceptance that the reversal of school integration, as first begun in

Figure 24. President William Jefferson Clinton in 1993.

the Nixon administration and accelerated by the Reagan administration, was a fait accompli. The notion of school integration was effectively left without a champion in the courts or at the ballot box.

There can be no doubt that the Clinton administration's attempt to promote and enforce civil rights was made narrower and in terms of school integration was ultimately inadequate. This in large part was due to the decisions of Republican presidencies since 1968 that were shaped by the realpolitik of the Southern Strategy. Viewed historically, Clinton's political capitulation signaled a retreat of the entire civil rights effort. Strict constructionist jurists, appointed in more than a dozen years of Republican control, reflected the views of the right and far right. In addition, after 1994 the GOP controlled both houses of Congress. Quite simply, the Clinton administration did not have the political will or strength to oppose the conservative array of institutional forces. During this era, Republican partisan maneuvers were explicitly in concert with the Southern Strategy. Clinton's response was to become a centrist and "triangulate" policies, which gained him political popularity while eroding any genuine movement to integrate the American classroom. As for affirmative action, rather than a full-throated endorsement, Clinton argued to "mend it, don't end it."[59] The Clinton record on civil rights was one of rhetorical advocacy coupled with the absence of a policy to integrate the public schools. At the end of his term Clinton announced a "conversation about race" and in 1998 held a roundtable to discuss "bipartisan solutions."[60] As noble as the idea was then, the partisan divide had become reinforced due in part to an increasing racial isolation in neighborhoods and classrooms. The last great meeting place of American democracy (the public school) was becoming increasingly more separate and unequal as children attended racially isolated schools in an environment that tacitly accepted or even endorsed segregation.

Bill Clinton's Recognition of Resegregation in the 1990s

The presidencies of Johnson and Reagan both dealt decisively with the paradox of racial segregation in America with the political will, legislative policies, and judicial appointments to affect the practice of public education. Johnson did so to promote school integration and inclusion, Reagan to forward the termination of court-ordered integration and set the inevitable path to exclusion, racial isolation, and resegregation. As for Clinton, by the late 1990s he enunciated the clear pattern of increased racial isolation in the classroom. As Clinton ruefully remarked:

> For the first time since the 1950s, our schools in America are resegregating. The rollback of Affirmative Action is slamming shut the doors of higher education on a new generation, while those who oppose it have not yet put forward any other alternative.

Clinton noted, "Segregation is no longer the law, but too often separation is still the rule."[61] Bill Clinton had diagnosed a problem for which he politically could not articulate a solution. As previously noted, the tool of busing to promote greater diversity in the classroom was not part of Clinton's lexicon to achieve racial integration in America's public schools. Incidentally, in her run for the presidency in 2016, Hillary Clinton, like her husband, also recognized the problem of growing resegregation. In a speech in May of that election year to the NAACP she stated, "Our schools are more segregated than they were in 1968. We've got to reverse that. It's dangerous."[62] As with the presidency of Bill Clinton (1992–2000), no effective policies or programs to integrate the public schools were articulated by the next occupant of the White House—George W. Bush.[63]

George W. Bush Follows Reagan's Policies as Racial Isolation Builds

George W. Bush became president in 2001. Educational policies that ignored public school integration paralleled those of Ronald Reagan and George Herbert Walker Bush. Those policies in part were based on the Supreme Court decisions of the 1990s.[64] Reagan and Bush appointees consistently ordered the effective termination of programs that promoted racial integration in case after case. Later, the appointments of Chief Justice John Roberts and Justice Samuel Alito maintained the conservative majorities on the Supreme Court to effectively continue the work begun in the early 1980s that had the effect of resegregating the American classroom. George W. Bush never mentioned resegregation during his eight-year tenure in office.[65] The major themes of his polices were embedded in the No Child Left Behind Act of 2002. The Bush administration stated that the law was designed to maintain local control while expanding opportunities for American children to gain a quality education. There was to be no effort to integrate America's public schools; instead, the focus was to hopefully raise achievement. Among the metrics to be used were standardized test scores. Accordingly, the Bush administration was focused on annual testing, reporting disaggregated data, and disseminating school information. While the argument to test or not to test may have been controversial, there was now no real debate about integration or desegregation. The issue in political terms had become invisible. Although never declared formally, segregated public schools at the beginning of the twenty-first century had become the expected—and, in some cases, the desired—norm.

Obama Defeats Southern Strategy Even as School Resegregation Increases

Barrack Obama, the first African American president of the United States, was elected in 2008 amid a financial crisis blamed in part on banking deregulation. Obama won nearly 53 percent of the popular vote, and his 365 electoral votes were the highest since fellow Democrat Bill Clinton won 379 electoral votes in 1996. Obama's popular vote percentage was the greatest of any candidate since 1988. The conservative Southern Strategy had failed Republicans amid the grave financial crisis in 2008. In 2012, Obama was reelected amid a small but well-timed increase in the income growth rate. Even though the

Figure 25. President
George W. Bush in
2003.

Southern Strategy proved ineffective nationally in presidential politics in two
straight elections, the Republicans were still winning the majority of congressional races state by state. During President Obama's eight years in office the
Democrats lost over 900 state legislature seats, 12 governors, 69 House seats,
and 13 Senate seats. With depleted ranks of Democratic legislators at the
national level, the dual presidential victories by Obama in 2008 and 2012 did
not reverse education policies that continued to allow school resegregation.
In that sense, Obama's victories in 2008 and 2012 were predictably pyrrhic.
Certainly, Republican state legislatures that continued to grow in electoral
strength were not going to push for desegregated classrooms. Nor would
greater majorities of a Republican Congress allow approval of major presidential initiatives (in education or otherwise)—not even ones the Republicans previously authored. In many ways, the same policies that came into
being in the 1980s under the Justice Department's Civil Right Division, then
headed by William Bradford Reynolds, continued to dismantle the manda-

tory and voluntary school desegregation initiatives. Funding for programs to integrate public schools remained nonexistent.

Obama's specific policies identified teacher quality as a large factor working toward educational improvement. For example, a 2009 appropriations bill included an increase in funding for the Teacher Incentive Fund. This was a program available to state and local education agencies that provided funds for increased "performance-based" salaries for teachers and principals in high-need schools. The Obama administration also called for a reauthorization process for the No Child Left Behind Act and the Elementary and Secondary Education Act (ESEA). There was talk about "transformative education law." Nevertheless, separate and unequal schools that promoted racial isolation continued to be a stark reality that none of Obama's reforms dealt with directly. During Obama's eight years in office (2009–17), there was no political consensus, indeed there was no political will, to reverse the growing inequalities within American public schools. In fact, the Government Accountability Office reported on the lack of desegregation from 2000–2001 to the 2013–14 school year. It noted that, in the 2000–2001 school year, 9 percent of public schools had 75 percent or more black or Latinx students. In comparison, in the 2013–14 school year, the number increased to 16 percent of all public schools. During that time span (2000–2014) the number of racially isolated schools more than doubled, from 7,009 schools to 15,089 schools.[66]

Trump Triumphant and the Spread of the Southern Strategy

In 2017 Donald Trump was sworn in as the forty-fifth president of the United States. Trump's signature theme heralded a political restoration to "Make America Great Again"—a motto directly lifted from a Ronald Reagan speech on Labor Day 1980 and the theme of the 1980 Republican Convention ("Let's Make America Great Again"). Trump's stated admiration for Reagan and his distrust of government in general and the public schools in particular were reflected in his appointment to the office of secretary of education of Betsy De Vos, a billionaire philanthropist. Her biography revealed that she had never worked on state educational policy nor ran a public university or school district. In addition, she had never taught in a public school or college. Trump's secretary of education was a strong advocate of school vouchers. She was in favor of letting students attend private schools via public funding.

Figure 26. President
Barack Obama in
2009.

Indeed, a federal voucher program, with the stated expectation of giving low-income families more high-quality school options, with an estimated cost of $20 billion, was a Trumpian campaign promise.[67]

This promise was not based on a new concept. In 1955, Milton Friedman wrote in *The Role of Government in Education* concerning the paying of private school tuition via taxpayer monies. Friedman's stated aim was to increase competition among schools. This marketplace notion had the dual hope of not only increased student achievement but decreased education costs. Over six decades after Friedman's writings on this idea, there was considerable research on the efficacy of state voucher programs. A quarter century of data on the Milwaukee voucher program found that 41 percent of all private voucher schools operating in Milwaukee between 1991 and 2015 had failed. Failure was determined by the closure of those schools. Further-

Figure 27. President Donald Trump in 2017.

more, the failure rate for entrepreneurial start-up schools was 67.8 percent. Other studies of school voucher programs have demonstrated mixed results on scores.[68] For example, while there have been negative effects in states like Louisiana and Indiana, there is evidence that showed higher reading and math scores for black students in New York City, and higher reading scores for students in the District of Columbia program.

Given this research on school voucher initiatives, under Trump's plan $20 billion of a present Department of Education budget of $70 billion would go to private schools, including religious schools. On the other hand, public schools would almost certainly lose some of their funding from state and federal coffers. Public schools would continue to serve millions of disadvantaged students, along with a student demographic characterized in part by family poverty and classrooms ever more segregated by race. In 2017, 170,000 students were on voucher programs. If extended to every student of low-income parents—which is Trump's ultimate plan—the program would encompass about 11 million students. If and when this came to pass it would mean approximately $110 billion toward vouchers—enough for every child living in poverty to have a scholarship of $12,000 toward the school presumably of his or her choice. There is, of course, the question, when a student chooses a private school with a federal voucher, of whether that school must accept that pupil. Historically, private schools are more likely than public schools to be much more discriminatory. If we define a school as all white when 90 percent or more of its students are white, enrollment patterns become evident. Forty-three percent of private school students in the United States attend virtually all white schools as compared to 27 percent of public school students in the nation.[69]

Early in the Trump administration, states' rights seemed to triumph over civil rights—two philosophies of governance that have been historically opposed. President Obama's Every Student Succeeds Act, one of the last pieces of legislation passed under Obama, was predictably overridden by a Republican Congress. Obama's education legislation had quite a historical pedigree that dated back to 1965. Recall that the Elementary and Secondary Education Act became law as a part of President Lyndon B. Johnson's War on Poverty. That law, born out of the civil rights movement, prioritized equal access to education while emphasizing high standards and accountability. Since then the 1965 Elementary and Secondary Education Act was renewed via a congressional reauthorization every five years. For example, the reauthorization of ESEA under President George W. Bush occurred under the No Child Left Behind Act of 2001. ESEA was most recently reauthorized on 2015 as the Every Student Succeeds Act under President Obama. Under that 2015 legislation students had to take standardized tests in math, reading, and science, and schools needed to report the progress of at-risk groups (e.g., disabled students, nonwhite students, and those learning English). The House of Representatives and the Senate in 2017 overturned the rules and federal regulations from the Obama era and President Trump signed off on them. This left ESEA as the law, but Secretary of Education Betsy DeVos gained the ultimate power on how to apply it. The sense of the Congress was clearly to reestablish state and local control over education across the nation. The Trump administration encouraged schools and colleges to pursue race-blind admissions standards, ending an Obama-era guideline meant to bolster diversity.[70]

One measurement of the importance of an educational policy initiative for a presidential administration can be found in the ongoing emphasis on educational issues from year to year in the president's State of the Union addresses. These annual reports to the country stem from Article II, Section 3 of the U.S. Constitution, which declares that the president "shall from time to time give to the Congress Information of the State of the Union, and recommend to their Consideration such measures as he shall judge necessary and expedient." In his first Joint Address to Congress , President Trump, per the official White House transcript (2017), mentioned education only twice. He noted, "Education is the civil rights issue of our time. (Applause.) I am calling upon members of both parties to pass an education bill that funds school choice for disadvantaged youth, including millions of African American and Latino children. (Applause.)"[71] To single out education as the civil rights issue of our time was extraordinary. However, promoting school choice (e.g., private charter schools) was problematic because charter schools have been and continue to be an institutional model known to be far more segregated than public schools.[72] Although Trump again mentioned education twice in his 2018 State of the Union, neither reference (using personal tax cut money for a child's education and education as a requirement for citizenship) dealt directly with federal education policy. In the 2019 State of the Union, Trump failed to mention education a single time in his 5,600 word, one hour and 20-minute speech. The emphasis on national educational policy between the years 2017 to 2019 in the State of the Union addresses were limited or nonexistent. Nevertheless, in 2019, one of the most conspicuous elements of President Trump's proposed federal education budget included a plan to create $5 billion in annual tax credits to provide a funding base for proposed Education Freedom Scholarships. These dollar-for-dollar tax credits would pay for private school scholarships as well as transportation, special education services, and more. Private schools, notably more segregated than the public schools, would continue to set their own admissions policies. In his 2020 State of the Union, Trump promoted his plans for school choice, high school vocational and technical education, and funding for historically black colleges and universities. He never mentioned public schools by name, instead referred to them as failing government schools.

From LBJ to Trump: Segregation to Desegregation to Resegregation

Kevin Phillips's brilliant and controversial analysis of the political landscape of 1969 in his landmark book, *The Emerging Republican Majority*, is seminal to understanding not just the last half of the twentieth century in American politics, but pivotal to comprehending trends that reach well into the twenty-first century. The Southern Strategy transformed both the Democratic Party and the Republican Party in the 1960s. A century after the election of Abraham Lincoln, the party of Lincoln became a states' rights political force. Republicans, like the Democrats and Dixiecrats before them, garnered southern votes based on notions of white supremacy and white resentment. This was done in part by using at times a thinly veiled code that substituted ideas on states' rights and a limited federal government for what was clearly a segregationist platform. That helped Richard Nixon become president in 1969.

Moreover, the Southern Strategy had over time become a national strategy as evidenced by electoral maps indicating the overwhelming support among white voters across large swaths of the nation for Republican candidates for both federal and state offices. Of course, at the heart of white supremacy and white resentment is the primal issue of race. Nixon's strategy as chronicled early on by Phillips had its genesis as the Democrats fought a split in their southern ranks in 1948. Although the Dixiecrat movement was short lived, over the long haul its ideology morphed into a southern faction—arguably now the heart and soul of the Republican Party. The *Brown* decision in 1954, the Civil Rights Act of 1964, and Voting Rights Act of 1965 kindled a backlash that continued to grow among the largest electoral group—the white voter—even into the twenty-first century. The Southern Strategy began as a regional political wedge in the South for Republicans in 1964, and this states' rights philosophy fostered school resegregation as it became the new normal in the latter part of the twentieth century and the beginning of the twenty-first century. That same Southern Strategy, as Phillips had predicted a half century ago, has become a successful national political strategy. As public school classrooms across the nation become ever more segregated, a fertile ground for racial stereotypes and bigotry produces a greater and greater social divide. Apartheid both fosters and depends on a racially divided populace. The undeniable statistical reality of public school and community resegregation only exacerbates growing political and social polarization.

Taking into consideration the understandably emotional issue of desegregation and without understanding the political history of national school legislation, one might expect that there would be an ongoing pitched battle over school resegregation. Yet the idea of public school integration had become all but invisible. Since the Reagan administration's *A Nation at Risk* report painted a picture of failing schools, each succeeding president promoted new plans to close the racial academic achievement gap that were essentially devoid of direct attempts to integrate the public schools. Thus, each president was attacking a symptom—a racial gap in achievement. None of them felt it politically wise to go to the heart of the actual problem, namely that separate and unequal schools are inherently a pernicious choice in a pluralistic democracy. No matter how well intentioned, Bill Clinton's Goals 2000, George W. Bush's No Child Left Behind Act, and Barack Obama's Every Student Succeeds Act were bound to be inherently inadequate.

For the last half century, school integration has been essentially a phantom issue, which cannot seem to find its way into the public consciousness or teacher education curricula. Politically speaking, since the 1970s the desegregation issue has had no voice, no powerful constituency, no national champion. The out of sight and out of mind phenomena appeared out of place—an anachronism, the issue of a bygone age. Yet the destructive effect of a separate and unequal school system does not only affect African American and Latinx students. It touches every child in two ways. First, separate and unequal schooling fundamentally fails to develop the social skills based on student-to-student interactions among children of different backgrounds to live and succeed in a diverse society. Second, separate and unequal schooling implicitly teaches that segregation is normal. An environment based on ignorance of others can be easily manipulated into misunderstanding, bias, fear, and even hate for those outside of one's personal social sphere. This traditional injustice based on racism has been and continues to be visited on generation to generation. Because the public school is the last great gathering place of democracy, the opportunity to build a united yet diverse community continues to be forsaken. From police shootings to social and economic restrictions on where a person can live and worship, there is a devolution into becoming a nation of strangers separated by race.

There are reasons the United States, more segregated today than it has been in 60 years, has botched the kind of school integration that the *Brown* decision envisioned in the mid-1950s. One dominant root cause is the political influence of the power of the presidency. Through the president nominating judges to be approved by the Senate, the future decisions of any federal court in the land can be affected. Knowing that the judiciary was playing a central role in the integration of schools in the 1960s, Richard Nixon's deal with archconservative Senator Strom Thurmond of South Carolina was a case study in how the promise of a "strict constructionist" judiciary could eventually change the trajectory of court decisions from pro-desegregation to

anti-desegregation. Specifically, a political deal was struck for the 1968 presidential campaign where Nixon promised the South that he would appoint
only "strict constructionists" to the federal judiciary (Warren E. Burger). In
addition, Nixon would nominate a southerner to the Supreme Court (Clem-
ent Haynsworth and G. Harrold Carswell—although both were rejected
by the Senate), come out against court-ordered busing, and pick someone
acceptable to the South for the vice presidency (Maryland's governor Spiro
Agnew). Nixon's political Southern Strategy calculus proved to be quite valuable as he received critical southern conservative support for his 1968 election to the presidency.

Moreover, Nixon's campaign promises to change the political balance on
the Supreme Court and in district courts proved effective. The latter courts
have proved to be important because in *Brown v. Board of Education of
Topeka II* (1955) the Supreme Court assigned the obligation of desegregation
to district courts, ordering the lower courts to integrate the schools "with all
deliberate speed." The ambiguity of the notion of "with all deliberate speed"
proved historically fatal to the desegregation orders throughout the country.
It allowed, via a mixture of evasion, continual postponement, and outright
resistance, a blocking of the momentum of the national effort to desegregate
the public schools.[73] More to the point of the Nixonian appointments to the
federal bench, the historical record indicates that the judiciary did gradu-
ally pull back from school desegregation (*Millikin*) and restrict the ability of
school districts to devise integration plans.

Nixon's political deals via the Southern Strategy pointed the way for others, Republicans from Reagan to Trump, to gain political support in exchange
for future promises for strict constructionist judicial appointments. The very
notion that a court could order a school to desegregate eventually became
invalidated. In *Parents Involved in Community Schools v. Seattle School District No. 1* (2007) the Court opined that racial balancing does not consti-
tute a compelling state interest. The judicial transformation from the Warren
Court to the Roberts Court emanated in part from a half century string of
presidential campaign promises from Nixon through Trump to appoint strict
constructionists to the federal bench. Racial discrimination now appeared
to be an individual choice devoid of the need for court orders. Chief Justice
Roberts declared in a circular argument in the 40 final words of the *Parents
Involved* decision, "the way to stop discrimination on the basis of race is to
stop discriminating on the basis of race."[74]

Historical realities over time—if known—can dissolve popular myths

commonly found in what has become accepted terminology. One such mis-
nomer since the New Deal is the notion of de facto segregation. The idea
that twentieth-century segregation extending from the neighborhood to
the schoolroom is simply an unintended happenstance defies the historical
record.[75] In fact, effective de jure segregation beginning in the Franklin Roosevelt administration, which took hold especially during the great housing
shortage after the Second World War, was an explicit federal government
policy that via legislation funded racial segregation for housing in cities
across the nation. It was at its root a plan of racial isolation developed in the
Great Depression of the 1930s, which was dutifully carried out to a massive
extent in the 1940s by state and local governments across the country.[76]

The politics behind the federal government's public housing policy in
this critical part of the postwar period involved three political factions. First
were the conservative Republicans led by Robert Taft, who was known as
"Mr. Conservative." He believed that federal involvement with public housing was a form of socialism and therefore unacceptable. The second faction
were Southern Democrats or "Dixiecrats" who were openly and profoundly
segregationists. The third political players were the liberal Democrats led by
Illinois senator Paul Douglas and Senator Hubert Humphrey of Minnesota
who favored public housing to alleviate the great postwar housing shortage.
To understand the political potency of the segregationist position, one need
only revisit the 1949 congressional debate over President Harry Truman's
proposed legislation for a federally funded public housing program. In order
to put a halt to any government housing program and protect the private
sector housing industry, Taft, knowing the Southern Democrats would never
accept racial integration, developed a "poison pill" amendment. That amendment simply stated that the 1949 housing bill would not segregate due to race.
The liberal Democrats knew the housing bill would fail without the votes of
the segregationist wing of their party. The liberal Democrats caved. They reasoned that a bill with segregated housing was better than no bill at all. Thus,
they ended up voting against Taft's prointegration amendment and then tried
to explain their position. Senator Douglas said, "I should like to point out to
my Negro friends what a large amount of housing they will get under this
act. . . . I am ready to appeal to history and to time that it is in the best interests of the Negro race that we carry through the housing program as planned,
rather than put in the bill an amendment which will inevitably defeat it."[77]

In terms of the racial resegregation in twenty-first-century American
schools, twentieth-century decisions by the executive and legislative branches

of the federal government have been buttressed by the Supreme Court. Note the plurality opinion of Chief Justice John Roberts in *Parents Involved in Community Schools v. Seattle School District No. 1.*[78] The chief justice wrote that racial categorization of students (for purposes of administering a choice program) except to reverse explicit rules to segregate students by race was unconstitutional. Thus, a racially isolated school, according to the concurring opinion of Justice Clarence Thomas, that was the result of "any number of innocent private decisions, including voluntary housing choices,"[79] could not constitutionally seek a remedy. Accordingly, even a voluntary desegregation plan under those conditions was not permissible.

The problem with the court's opinion in 2007 was its ahistorical premise. Since the New Deal, de jure (as a matter of law) discrimination has been the operative mode to explicitly segregate neighborhoods, which in turn led directly to segregated schools.[80] From the 1940s on, de facto segregation might well be termed so-called "de facto" segregation. Since the 1930s, when Harold Ickes, President Roosevelt's first public housing director, determined that public housing should not disturb the preexisting racial composition of neighborhoods, de jure segregation has been in effect. What was then termed the "neighborhood composition rule"[81] established a precedent with profound consequences to maintain segregation where it existed and extend segregation where it had not.[82] The rule basically required that tenants of a housing development would be of the same race as the population of the area where the housing was located. The downstream effect of Ickes's policy, created in the early Roosevelt administration, led to the federally subsidized relocation of whites to suburbs, while at the same time did not now allow similar arrangements for African Americans. The residue of the policies and practices of the federal government decades ago remain, as evidenced by the racially isolated neighborhoods and schools in the 2020s.

Given the political and pedagogical stakes, one might hope that schools and colleges of education would produce curricula that examines the issue of historical segregation and recognizes growing resegregation. A curricular framework of principles, policies, and practices to encourage integrated classrooms would be conceptualized as a professional responsibility. The marginalization of the reality of resegregation in the press, political discourse, and our college and university teacher education programs has muted or even silenced local, regional, and national awareness of resegregation. A more focused and robust method of understanding solution sets within the teaching profession seems imperative both for new teacher programs as well as teacher in-service training. A dialogue among educators to identify and promote ideas that forward the ideal of school integration appears to be a good place to start. Although new curricula for teacher education cannot battle resegregation alone, it is a good first step to enlighten educators. Part 3 of this book outlines the pedagogical options to desegregate the American classroom.

PART 3

Pedagogical Plans to Desegregate America's Classrooms

Figure 28. "I have a dream that one day down in Alabama . . . little black boys and little black girls will be able to join hands with little white boys and little white girls as sisters and brothers."—Martin Luther King Jr.

Desegregation of Public Schools in the Twenty-First Century

The first and second sections of this book outlined the continuing historical and political record of an ongoing battle between the forces of inclusion via integration as opposed to exclusion via segregation in the American public school. An excellent question as to why the various separate state governments did not devise effective policies to desegregate public education on a statewide basis begs for an answer. To supply a rejoinder, two amendments to the United States Constitution must be understood. To begin, there can be little question that the Tenth Amendment to the Constitution provides the basis in legal theory for making education a primary function of the various states. The salient constitutional passage states, "The powers not delegated to the United States by the Constitution, nor prohibited by it to the States, are reserved to the States respectively, or to the people." Of course, the Constitution can be and has been revised since 1789. Thus, while education has not been historically regarded as a "fundamental right" under the Constitution, the equal protection clause of the Fourteenth Amendment (1868) affects the Tenth Amendment in that it mandates when a state establishes a public school system, no child living in that state may be denied equal access to schooling. Thus, the merging of the Tenth and the Fourteenth Amendments yields the notion of state control of equal access to schooling, which under *Plessy* (1896) allowed for *separate but equal* public schools. The Supreme Court overturned the practice of *separate but equal* in the *Brown*, (1954) ruling, declaring that state laws establishing separate public schools for black and white students are unconstitutional.

Given the previous historical and constitutional background one might assume that it was a state's right—indeed, a duty—at least since 1954 to provide integrated equal access to public schools for all. Yet the historical record shows that none of the states made significant strides to provide what these states had the right and obligation to extend to an ever-expanding school populace. In a sense, a demonstration of the inadequacy of state action was embodied in the very need for Title VI of the Civil Rights Act of 1964, which protected people from discrimination based on race, color, or national origin in programs or activities (e.g., public schools) that received federal financial assistance. As has been preciously outlined, the "carrot and stick" approach from President Johnson pointed out that integrated schools would receive federal funds, while segregated schools would not. This strategy worked well to help desegregate schools: from a completely segregated school starting point in the South of the early 1960s, about 90 percent of black children attended desegregated schools by the early 1970s.[1] Of course, with the election of Ronald Reagan in 1980, the federal government reversed course on desegregation. Still, the question remains, why did not the states as political entities ever take the initiative to desegregate their schools? Why was the major reaction to *Brown* the rise of states' rights political organizations from the Klan and the Dixiecrats in the South to hypocritical politicians of historically segregated schools in the North—who were only too eager to point the finger of blame at the de jure segregation of southern states, while ignoring what had been termed de facto segregation in their own communities? Why the rejection of meaningful civil rights progress not only in the states' schools but in society in general—from public accommodations to fair housing? In short, why did the states (North and South) uniformly use their Tenth Amendment authority and disregard their Fourteenth Amendment responsibility when it came to basic civil rights? The answer may be found in the politically decentralized structure that begins with local electorates in cities and towns across America, whose private inclinations and deliberate public policies fashioned state and eventually national inaction, which in turn produced a society ever more segregated.[2]

As has been noted in the United States there is an intentional stratification of good schools, pristine public parks, clean water, and professional police forces to protect the citizenry. Some neighborhoods and cities have these advantages, others clearly do not.[3] The quality of life residents experience is dependent, to a great extent, on the segregated communities in which they reside. There are two sides to the segregation coin. One side represents the poor and people of color in housing locations isolated from the reverse side of the coin, namely relatively wealthy white residents who live in neighborhoods replete with resources needed to maintain a high quality of community life. Demographic trends and historical expenditures indicate strongly that cities have inequitably and intentionally, since the early part of the twentieth century, provided for services in ways that both promoted and maintained segregation.[4] Districts' and neighborhoods' land use (e.g., sewage systems, garbage collection, paved and regularly serviced streets) were provided with purposely unequal allocations of resources as communities were planned and zoned. Politically potent white homeowner neighborhoods and business properties were purposely designed to be exclusive in order to provide a heavily concentrated delivery of public goods to these politically powerful constituents.[5] Quite literally, residential zones were drawn and restrictive covenants were issued to assure that the distribution of municipal services and well-funded schools occurred unevenly to the benefit of the wealthy white class. This process created segregated enclaves and segregated schools to maintain a system of social replication that exists to the present day. In addition, too often the phenomena of white flight from the cities to the suburbs renewed and reinforced the isolation of races and further separated the poor from the wealthy, which is to say nonwhites from whites. The myth, still accepted in many corners, that segregation was the residue of individual preferences is belied by a history of public record from city and town councils to zoning and redevelopment boards.[6]

Correspondingly, the notion that individual bad actors (e.g., predatory bankers and landlords) were the only culprits that caused the racial isolation of African Americans in major cities belies the historical record.[7] Actually, there exists a litany of consistent federal, state, and local policies that promoted American residential segregation from the 1930s to the twenty-first century. For example, segregated public housing projects emanating from President Franklin Roosevelt's New Deal endorsed state-sanctioned racial discrimination. These federal actions were followed by racial zoning ordinances enacted by city governments. To attempt to justify this unconstitutional racial segregation, there arose a widespread assumption that property values would decline if African Americans purchased homes in white neighborhoods. Here it must be noted that the Federal Housing Administration had no evidence of this claim, and in fact had findings to the contrary. Such discriminatory practices over the decades opened the door to banks and mortgage lenders to concoct a plan known as reverse-redlining (i.e., targeting minority communities for clearly exploitative subprime loans). When the housing bubble burst in 2008, middle-class and lower-middle-class African American and Latinx communities unable to pay their home loans were devastated.[8] A decade later, white home ownership stood at 71 percent compared to 41 percent black home ownership. This race-based ownership gap was greater than in 1900.[9] For white and black families of modest means, owning a home is the major source of wealth. In contemporary America, the downstream effect of generational discriminatory practices created, in part, an economic class structure based on race. In 2018, the median black family had a net worth of $3,400 compared to the median white family net worth of $140,000.[10]

Clearly, urban segregation happens on an unequal playing field. Local governments have historically selected preordained neighborhood winners and losers by augmenting selected property values through transferring municipal and county resources toward selected neighborhoods prioritized by wealth. It has been said that all politics is local. The inability of states to create and maintain fair and equitable school systems throughout the nation has been due to a linked political reality. State governments generate political power from a decentralized system that begins with the local electorate. Local political activity is largely about the politics of land use.[11] Land use has been the central concern of white property owners who seek to enhance their economic position and control the allocation of services by means of the use of local property taxes intended to fund public education. Wealthy neighborhoods simply draw on a more robust property tax base to produce better funded public schools. The use of zoning and redevelopment planning has greatly aided in a deliberate system of segregated communities. The United States is the only country in the world where the value of its schools is calculated by the real estate value of the homes that it serves. Finally, it is not as though the Tenth Amendment is not a factor in state education. History demonstrates that it has been used to stall or simply ignore civil rights remedies and judicial rulings by the federal court system. It is a simple political reality that actions that emanate from local school boards, zoning districts, and city councils have and continue to benefit white property owners and their allies, resulting in a dearth of significant state activity to provide equal access to a quality education for all its citizenry. The overarching reality is that residential segregation leads to school segregation. Although school choice programs have gained notoriety, most children attend school in their residential neighborhood. If a neighborhood is not integrated, in all probability the school will not be. It is estimated that neighborhood segregation is the root cause of about three-quarters of school segregation across cities.[12]

From the 1970s to the present day, pedagogic research has continued to point to "bumpy" yet slowly shrinking achievement gaps between children of color and other students.[13] Researchers have noted the strongest correlates of achievement gaps to be racial/ethnic differences in parents' income, parents' education, and racial/ethnic segregation.[14] As has been pointed out, any number of presidential initiatives such as Goals 2000, the No Child Left Behind Act, and the Every Student Succeeds Act have prescribed ways to improve achievement for all students and yet all have been complicit in accepting a public school system that is each day for the last two generations more separate and unequal. As well intentioned as these various national policies and programs may have been, given that they did not identify resegregation as a core problem to quality education, they have merely attacked the symptoms (e.g., low standardized test scores of children of color) and not the causes of what has been called a de facto apartheid public school system in a society increasingly segregated by race and class. This failure to view school racial integration as a solution, among federal and state policy makers, and to search for political/pedagogic solution sets that do not take it into account appears to ignore the fact that during the 1960s and 1970s the racial differences in achievement gaps at the height of school integration were at their most narrow.[15] Clearly there is a need to solve the pedagogical-political paradox that proves that a diverse school population benefits all children and the long-standing political consensus that nothing can—or even should be done—to integrate the public schools. Derrick Darby and John Rury point out that school leaders, first, have an obligation each day to bring justice and dignity to each student by first—inside the classroom—acknowledging systemic manifestations of the historically mistaken idea of innate "racial differences" in the areas of cognitive ability and social behavior.[16] Second, beyond the classroom, it is part of the ethical responsibility of every teacher to mitigate the known negative effects of generational grinding poverty, growing school segregation, and an enduring societal inequality that can harm academic achievement and social growth. Understanding that public schools are vital to the strength of American democracy and that quality schools are dependent on excellent teachers, it is appropriate to ask how teacher education programs can help to reverse school resegregation and make a breakthrough to establish a national consensus to promote racially diverse schools.

After understanding the premise that, in a pluralistic democracy, children grow academically and develop socially best in a diverse learning environment, it seems appropriate that teacher education programs at the college and university level should retool their curricula. The focus of new core curricula should be, in part, to have teacher candidates understand the historical and political realities of resegregation, then comprehend how to provide professional leadership in moving their communities and schools in a direction that best provides a quality education for all students. Realizing that in a democratic society there can be no quality education for students in a separate and unequal system, it is past time to revise the traditional myopic course work in K–12 teacher education. Teacher education too often has focused on narrow student achievement measures, various and changing state standards

Figure 29. An inclusive educational institution holds the promise of a new type of twenty-first-century school—a place of expanding knowledge that views diversity of language, thought, and culture as a learning opportunity.

in the 50 states, while fundamentally ignoring the social context of growing resegregation in the public schools. Such new teacher education curricula should not be embedded in a single course but should provide a centerpiece for an entire program leading to a teacher education certificate or a master's degree in education, or both. In short, the path to becoming a quality teacher in twenty-first-century America begins with the basic understanding that public school integration by race and socioeconomic status can benefit every child. To transform growing racial segregation into an integrated environment, enlightened teachers and administrators need not only to explain to school board members, parents, and students the pedagogic reasons for and the benefits of integrated schools, but how to achieve the goal of a diverse quality learning environment for every student.

Let us understand that for the first time in our nation's history that the majority of K-12 students in public schools are children of color. That clearly indicates that demographically the United States is becoming a very different country than the nation of past generations. Between 1968 and 2011, the

United States experienced a 28 percent decline in white public school enrollment, at the same time there was a 495 percent increase in the number of
Latinx students.[17] The great misfortune of the last four decades is that as the
school population has become more diverse it has become more racially isolated. African American students in the South and West are now more segregated than they were in the late 1980s and 1990s. In California racial isolation
is such that Latinx students have less contact with white students than with
other students diverse ethnic or racial backgrounds.[18]

It is historically important to realize that at one time the American public
school was being successfully desegregated. Desegregation during the 1970s
proved effective, using tools such as busing, integrating schools, and quite
meritoriously narrowing the achievement gap among white students and
students of color. The progress of those years remain archived quietly in the
annals of history in spite of the sheer enormity of the change.[19] They failed
to sufficiently point out not only the social advantages but also the academic
benefits of public schools that reflected the American demographic reality.
Now in the second decade of the twenty-first century it is imperative that
the rationale for integration be understood and appreciated by all the stakeholders (parents, teachers, students, administrators, school board members,
community residents, and state as well as national leaders). The urgency to
become fully aware of the breadth and depth of the challenge of desegregation
and the inherent cognitive and social value of an integrated school falls to all
informed leaders, but in a very special way to those in higher education who
would innovate and modernize enlightened teacher education programs.

The Pedagogic Case for Racial Integration

There is a plethora of research that indicates that integration by race and
socioeconomic status benefits all children. Over a half century ago, in 1966,
the congressionally authorized Coleman Report made it clear that integration
benefits student achievement. Since then, despite local, state, and national
intransigence against ending school segregation, there has been a large body
of consistent research from social science to support the notion that school
integration is good for all children. Let us be clear, it is important for scholars
in the field of pedagogy and especially teacher education programs to point
out that ignoring the social science research on the negative effects of segregated schools makes it not only improbable to close large achievement gaps

Figure 30. The effects of such racially integrated classrooms are multigenerational.

among students of different races and promote social development for every student, but makes segregation a multigenerational reality.

Every K-12 teacher should be aware of the research regarding students who are in a working relationship with other learners from diverse backgrounds. Studies indicate students attain improved cognitive abilities, including those skills that never become obsolete: critical thinking and problem-solving skills.[20] Students who enter into productive classroom relationships within an integrated school simply learn better to communicate, negotiate, and problem solve with people from different backgrounds.[21] Such abilities in the second decade of the twenty-first century are critical as we continue to note both historical and recent events (e.g., hate crimes, use of deadly force, racial profiling, rioting) where racial injustice for many Americans seems to have been normalized. It would appear necessary that there should be a realization of the pernicious effects of resegregation, especially among local, state, and national K–12 educational policy makers, as well as teacher education programs. All engaged in the teaching and learning enterprise should understand that resegregated schools from which prejudice and stereotypes emanate and fester not only reflect societal indifference and even the promotion of discrimination, but act to regenerate forms of apartheid that grow from generation to generation.

The Cognitive Benefits of a Diverse Learning Environment

Edified leaders must comprehend the benefits of ending racial isolation and beginning anew to integrate the American classroom. Let us start with the notion that integrated schools generate a powerful synergy where an inherent respect for the talent and worth of every student can produce optimal academic achievement and social growth essential for a vibrant multicultural democracy. In short, students have found it invaluable.[22] As has been noted, there is an array of recent findings indicating the efficacy of integrated schooling for various groups of students. For African Americans, school desegregation "significantly increased both educational and occupational attainments, college quality and adult earnings, reduced the probability of incarceration, and improved adult health status; desegregation had no effects on whites across each of these outcomes."[23] This falls in line with much of the social science research on school desegregation, which shows mixed test score results with a positive trend toward higher African American student achievement that happened during the aforementioned peak years of desegregation. In addition, there have been documented long-term academic and professional gains for African American adults who attended racially mixed schools. A 2004 study, *How Desegregation Changed Us: The Effects of Racially Mixed Schools on Students and Society*, attempted to connect personal perspectives about desegregation from different schools and towns systematically. This investigation attempted to answer whether the struggles to desegregate the public schools were worth the trouble. In that research foray, more than 500 graduates, educators, advocates, and local policy makers were interviewed, representing the voices of those directly involved in integrated public schools. This five-year study revealed that desegregation created an environment that made the vast majority of the students who attended integrated schools less racially prejudiced. These students said they were more comfortable around people of different backgrounds. Significantly and unfortunately after high school, these former students have lived far more segregated lives in a society that continues to become ever more racially isolated. To sum up, the overwhelming opinion of nearly every interview among African Americans, whites, Latinxs, and Asians was that desegregation formed their views about race and helped them overcome fear and distrust of people who were different.[24]

Research indicated that when students attended integrated classrooms, the outcomes were beneficial to all students.[25] Correspondingly, there was evidence of reduced testing gaps among students of different backgrounds, not because white student achievement went down, but because African American and Latinx student achievement increased. Historically, it is a significant yet simple fact that the K-12 gap in racial achievement closed more swiftly during the peak years of desegregation in the 1970s and early 1980s than at any time after that when desegregation policies fell out of political favor from the 1980s to the present day.[26] What in large measure has replaced meaningful school desegregation policies is the notion of school accountability—promoting the idea that providing instruction to every student via state standards will reduce achievement gaps as demonstrated through standardized test scores. On the whole that has not happened.[27]

Neglecting a call for desegregation over the last two generations has led to public education policies that have unwittingly or intentionally introduced an era of *neo-Plessyism*, where separate and unequal schools have not only endured but have grown. Further research indicates that, on average, better academic outcomes occur, regardless of child poverty, when students attend socioeconomically and racially diverse schools as compared with students in schools with concentrated poverty.[28] Moreover, other studies reveal that higher test scores are earned by students in integrated schools than in high-poverty schools. Segregation is tied to poverty. High-poverty schools are, on average, much less academically effective than lower-poverty schools.[29] In addition, students attending integrated schools are less likely to drop out and, not surprisingly, more likely to enroll in college. In terms of cognitive development, integrated classrooms are beneficial to all students due to the promotion of critical thought where students share their analysis, synthesis, and evaluation within a problem-solving environment.[30]

Affective Benefits of a Diverse Learning Environment

The affective domain refers to one's feelings, emotions, and values. How one feels about his or her environment (e.g., school) can virtually open or close the door to learning.[31] The affective benefits of social interaction seem inherent in an untracked, integrated school. However, a school must promote a level of cultural competency to present an optimum environment for students to develop academically and grow socially. Creating a friendly environment in an integrated school by involving all students not only in the

Figure 31. Integrated schools are an obvious remedy to discriminatory attitudes and prejudices born of isolation and ignorance.

most enriched curricular experience but also in extracurricular activities is a pathway to genuinely reaching a peak level of academic growth and social development.[32] The lack of racial isolation allows for students to have peers of diverse backgrounds. Correspondingly, there is opportunity with the guidance of informed teachers and staff to experience a learning environment of cross-cultural social interactions including meaningful conversations about race and identity. More than just increase tolerance, an integrated school can demonstrate daily evidence of the inaccuracy of racial and ethnic stereotypes.

Again, it is important for today's American educators to know that desegregated schools fundamentally change those who have experienced them. Given a diverse school population, students can learn to be more secure and confident and therefore more likely to appreciate and be open to integrated environments in neighborhoods, at work, and in social settings as they become adults. In addition, desegregation has been shown to make the vast majority of students less racially prejudiced and more comfortable with people of different backgrounds.[33] Working and collaborating with a diverse group of students can lead to greater self-efficacy among all students. In other words, a "can do" attitude based on intellectual self-confidence is a by-product of success in an integrated learning environment. To reiterate, the vast majority of graduates from desegregated schools, regardless of racial and ethnic background, greatly valued the daily cross-racial interaction in their high schools.[34] Accordingly, an integrated school provides a gateway to preparing students for the world of work in a diverse global economy.[35] Working within a diverse study body can promote collaboration and partnerships among people from very different backgrounds, which is a skill that has long-term societal advantages.

Given the intransigence of the political process toward promoting school integration as the best way to educate children in a democracy, we must ask more of our schools and colleges of education and ultimately our teachers than what educators have delivered in the past. The knowledge of America's policies and practices seen through the prism of a historical, political, and pedagogical lens is crucial for today's three million public school educators. These teachers who serve in 100,000 public schools have a paramount role to play to integrate the American classroom. The contradiction of segregation within a democracy can only be solved via the recognition that surging resegregation is a reality and that for educators at any level to be unaware or simply ignore it is professional negligence. Once this is understood, twenty-first-century action plans designed by America's best and brightest educators to truly integrate the nation's schools can become the inevitable future.

Paradox of Segregation and the Negligence of Scholars

In a multiracial democratic society, it seems inherently obvious that a segregated school system is an anathema. The classic battle between states' rights (promoting segregation) and civil rights (supporting integration) has been fought in state legislatures and the halls of Congress through the twentieth and now into the twenty-first centuries. The theory of racial separation in the United States is as old as the federal constitution and has been historically maintained via laws (de jure segregation) and court decisions (e.g., *Plessy v. Ferguson* in 1896). After 1954, unfortunately, so-called de facto segregation continued and grew within the nation that proclaimed the goal of integration without the national consensus to achieve it. Acceptance of racial separation for many has become the norm, and integration remains "a distant and unreachable goal."[36]

We have seen that except for a brief period in the 1960s and 1970s racial separation in schools and neighborhoods has appeared to be intractable throughout the nation. A separate and unequal school system endures for a myriad of reasons that do not directly involve politicians or members of the judiciary. One of the reasons for a separate and unequal public school system is the negligence of scholars in general and schools and colleges of education in particular to take the initiative to teach and promote school integration as a professional responsibility. This is not to say that valuable scholarship has not been done as it relates to social justice extending to the American class-room. This book has been constructed in part on the outstanding work and insight of many scholars. The problem is that theory has *not* affected practice. Those who have the responsibility to set academic curricula in teacher edu-cation programs in the colleges and universities across the nation, and the bodies or agencies that accredit them, have not done enough. It is imperative that teacher education programs ensure that the new vanguard of teacher candidates are aware of growing resegregation and, moreover, focus curricula to develop school and community plans to remedy the situation via new and creative ways to integrate America's schools. This must be conceptualized as a fundamental professional duty.

Achieving the reality of genuine societal racial emancipation and anti-subordination begins with the realization that the nation is not now nor has it ever been a color-blind society and is certainly not presently in a postracial era.[37] It has been noted repeatedly that the public school is more racially iso-lated now than in generations—with all signs pointing to greater segregation. Until there is a focus on the unfairness and immorality of racial inequality, the reproduction of a segregated society can only accelerate. Within an oppres-sive system, certain racist assumptions become widespread. For example, the assumption that minority and low-income children will do poorly on stan-dardized tests seems commonplace. It has been called the soft bigotry of low expectations. Actually, there is nothing soft about such bigotry. The simple statistical fact is that more and more minority and low-income students go to separate and unequal schools.[38] The acceptance of a predetermined out-come based on race has become normalized. It has found acceptance among too many from the elementary school yard to the graduate school semi-nar. For many decades, we have known that the differences in achievement demonstrated among students of culturally and racially distinct backgrounds as compared to white students are not the result of differences in ability to learn. Rather, they are in large part the result of inherently unfair separate and unequal schooling that exists across the nation. This is not to say that other factors do not exist. High crime rates, the illegal sale and use of mind-altering drugs, and grinding generational poverty are also a reality that extends into the classroom. However, these pernicious elements are inevitably linked to segregated communities. It is a myth to think that communities and school boards that draw the boundaries are not complicit in effectuating racial isolation.[39] As bleak as the current situation appears, there is evidence on which to base a renewed call for school integration in terms of the benefits to both the students of today and the society of tomorrow. Jonathan Kozol maintains that those who do not openly affirm the need for integrated schools, but instead devise compensatory programs to lessen the racial opportunity gap by asking more of the resegregated public schools, misinterpret of the legacy of Brown by unwittingly upholding the remnants of *Plessy*. In short, and they are fundamentally unaware of the core mission of the civil rights movement of the mid-twentieth century and the transformational vision of Dr. King.[40]

Solution Sets to Desegregation in the 2020s

Bringing about integrated public schools is about creating open-minded partnerships across multiple sectors from states, big cities, small towns, and their local school boards. To be clear, those partnerships and collaborations to devise solution sets to curtail current racial isolation in our communities, and subsequently our schools, are in dire need of national, state, and local policies as in the 1960s and 1970s that viewed integration as a social good. However, such a revival needs a fertile ground from which to grow. Therefore, the seminal work for desegregated schools falls heavily on universities and colleges in general—and schools and colleges of teacher education programs in particular. Such efforts will require a dedicated mission to prioritize school integration. Schools and colleges of education in the twenty-first century must comprehend the need for innovation, understand that instruction can occur onsite or online, plus grasp the value of cultural competency to assure public input from all members of a society ever more socially and linguistically diverse. Moreover, different approaches to desegregation need community consensus, action plans, and implementation. The solution sets can come from the merging of school districts, from creating open-enrollment magnet schools, or even mandating busing to achieve racial balance. In addition, twenty-first-century technologies can form part of the mix of creative solution sets. The central idea is that professional educators need to focus on new ways to promote both intraschool and interschool desegregation. Segregated schools within districts must end along with tracking within the walls of a school. This is no easy task. David Labaree reminds us that there is a long history of individual families using schools to preserve social advantage.[41] This in turn provides a host environment for social replication. Private interests can trump public policy when national and state goals are poorly conceived and executed or simply nonexistent.

Jonathan Kozol maintains that the federal government can accomplish significant headway in integrating the schools in a single year. The national government could provide an "irresistibly enticing package of incentives" that would allow wealthy schools located in the suburbs to admit inner-city children. Incentives might include additional per-pupil funding to support the inner-city transfers, construction funds to expand facilities, monies to recruit and employ advocates and mentors onsite to ensure the transition in both social and pedagogic realms, plus funds to underwrite student transportation by point-to-point travel from one specific urban neighborhood to one specific school.[42] The students of greatest need, as determined by low achievement scores and overcrowded schools, would receive priority. Kozol went on to note what has *not* worked in the past. Charter schools, which are publicly funded tuition-free schools of choice that are run independently, turn out to be even more segregated than most public schools.[43] Likewise, magnet schools, a public school offering a focus on distinctive programs not available elsewhere (e.g., social science, performing arts, humanities, mathematics, natural sciences), were designed to attract a more diverse student body within a school district, yet over the last half century they have not been effective in lessening the national trend toward greater school racial isolation.

Kozol's suggestions were akin to former secretary of education John King's 2016 plan. King, who was appointed to finish the last year of the Obama presidency as secretary of education, promoted the Stronger Together initiative. This plan, which would have needed congressional approval, would have more than doubled federal funding for school-integration efforts by targeting $120 million in competitive grants to districts that encouraged voluntary integration programs. This particular belated effort in 2016 never had a chance due to the political realities of the conservative majorities in Congress.

There are other concomitant long-range strategies that Erica Frankenberg and Gary Orfield have also noted including revisions to zoning laws that perpetuate racial isolation. To that end, Jessica Trounstine recommends that policy makers might reverse unjust systems of segregation in three specific ways. First, states could incorporate school districts and municipalities to assist in promoting integration and mitigating isolation. Second, states could subsidize lower income residents to allow them access to more neighborhoods and carefully construct multifamily housing away from economically marginal communities. Third, states could redistribute public goods in the manner that some states have already done for school funding.[44]

In short, there is a great need for housing integration in cities and at the same time a racial diversification of suburbs. This long-range policy can lead to less and less racial isolation in the public schools. This battle is outside the school, but progressive educators who see the promotion of civil rights as part of their professional responsibility should take an active role in informing their local governments of the advantages of school integration that would greatly aid in raising the quality of their public schools. City leaders and educators also need to have ongoing dialogues and action plans to locate attractive new schools in gentrified inner cities. This would be beneficial not only to cities and businesses, but to the social fabric of the nation. In addition, an upsurge in subsidized housing would give children enhanced access to schools. Such a reassignment of students to schools with the aforementioned incentives as outlined by Kozol could be integrated racially, socioeconomically, and linguistically with support staff to provide the most enriched curriculum taught via the widest variety of methodological approaches. These solution sets and other initiatives are imperative because, pedagogically, it is known that schools separated by race cannot consistently provide a quality education. Fundamentally, segregated schools are harmful to *all* children.[45]

Vital Role of Schools and Colleges of Education

Schools and colleges of education have an obligation to provide a twenty-first-century curricula that focuses on inclusion in today's ever more segregated society that presents the academically and socially harmful reality of exclusion. Understanding how American apartheid in the classroom is rationalized and a clinical comprehension of both the detrimental psychological and sociological effects of racial segregation are needed to best prepare new teachers for the kinds of schools in which most of them will practice. What are the kinds of courses that would populate such curricula? Duke University listed an offering named Segregation in Education: A Case of Back to the Future? This course presented a "timeline of United States segregation,

Figure 32. Integrated schools inherently afford every student access to the cultural competency and world-class education necessary to live, work, and succeed in America's multicultural tomorrow.

desegregation, integration and resegregation." Furthermore, it examined both historical and current policies and practices that pertain to opportunity, equality, and equity. Significantly, students engaged in a minimum of 20 hours of planned service activities.[46] Bates College listed a course titled Race, Cultural Pluralism, and Equality in American Education. It presented a "thematic investigation of school segregation, desegregation, and resegregation."[47] One course query asked, what would equal educational opportunity look like in a multicultural society? Likewise, Cornell College listed Education Policy and Practice. That offering reviewed "education policies and their relationship to sociological patterns of school resegregation, the rise of credentialism, the end of educational expansion, and inequality of educational opportunity." Also examined were demographic data on educational attainment, and an analysis of policies that either alleviated or reinforced educational inequality.[48]

While these individual courses are laudatory, what is called for perhaps is an entire program or concentration on the inclusion/exclusion paradox.

It is critical that new teachers examine the historical, legal, psychological, political, sociological, and pedagogical components of the reality of racial isolation via the resurgence of resegregation in the nation's public schools. As has been noted, knowledge of past structured inequality permits one to more fully understand an archetypal flaw (e.g., proclaiming inclusion while practicing exclusion) in American education. This comprehension can also provide a context to seek solutions in the teaching and learning enterprise. While no single pedagogical policy can change centuries-old structured inequality in the American public school, a judicious mix of well-articulated policies, programs, and practices is needed that emanate from a historical, political, and pedagogical context of what has worked in the past and via new technologies what can be effective in the future. Many teacher education programs are in dire need of curricular adjustments to best prepare today's teacher candidates for the unfortunate reality of segregated public school classrooms. Schools and colleges of education should be in the forefront of providing these soon to be new teachers with the awareness, knowledge, and cultural competence to begin to transform their community public school from an island of racial isolation to a citadel of inclusion.

Gender as a Marker of Difference

Part 1 of this book dealt with the blatant gender bias of the nineteenth century as women began to become school teachers. There were a plethora of sociocultural issues that shaped the teaching profession. From the formalization of schools, to the culture of benevolence, along with traditional gender stereotypes, evolving norms were fashioned and crystallized. Sadly, the residue of gender bias has endured for the vast majority of educators—women now make up over three-quarters of all elementary and secondary teachers in the nation's schools. Teaching in America has historically been and continues to be a relatively low paying and low social status profession that is inextricably linked to gender bias. Combined with a myriad of state-by-state credentialing regulations, the recruitment of new teachers is seen as problematic.[49]

Gender is a complex notion that deals in part with personal identity. The traditional issue of gender equality in the twenty-first century is no longer simply a binary struggle of a female quest for equity in a male-dominated world. Currently the issues of gender identity play out every day inside America's classrooms, which contain 50 million school children. In the contemporary school, traditional policies and practices concerning gender are in flux. What should remain constant is a philosophical commitment to provide a safe, caring, and yet challenging academic environment for all students regardless of gender distinctions. Supporting every student includes transgender (persons whose gender identity is viewed as distinct from their sex assigned at birth) and gender-expansive children (people with a broader gender identity than a culture's traditional definition of gender). Whether through intention or ignorance of the complex notion of gender, real harm can be done to students and the entire learning environment when a student becomes marginalized in a school.[50]

All stakeholders (superintendents, principals, parents, teachers, and the students themselves) need to possess not only the awareness of a new gender palate, but be committed to work in unison to provide a secure, supportive, and at the same time an academically challenging setting for every learner. For the twenty-first-century educator, just as with issues of race and class, there is a need to recognize that one's own traditional values may contain implicit or explicit biases, or both. The traditions of male dominance and white privilege negatively affect teaching and learning. The first step in the eradication of these fundamentally pernicious ideas depends on awareness of such prejudice. Understanding that gender-based discrimination in education is both a cause and a consequence of antiquated and harmful beliefs, customs, and mores is essential for their elimination from schools. These biases have no place in the classroom because of their divisive nature. Schools have a dual responsibility for academic growth and social development. Gender, racial, and class prejudice all stunt social development and negatively affect the learning of every student regardless of socioeconomic status, race, or gender identity. It is imperative for teachers to cultivate a classroom that actively promotes not only the acceptance but the celebration of the unique talents, abilities, and personal characteristics of every student.

Culturally Relevant Teaching and Learning

Tyrone Howard has pointed out that many times the notion of culture is misunderstood by professional educators as a factor relating to how students experience schools. Developing cultural competency—the ability to comprehend, communicate, and interrelate with people across cultures—is vital to

successful outcomes for all students, native-born and newcomer. It is important to note that cultural competence is not simply a black or white issue.
The American classroom is home to multiple cultures and language groups.[51]
Merely understanding the idea of cultural competency is necessary but not
sufficient for today's professional educator. Three ways to demonstrate cultural competency in the classroom are to (1) drop the traditional notion of the
classroom as a place for cultural amalgamation; (2) view culturally and linguistically different students as a resource and not a liability while developing
a culturally sustaining pedagogy; and (3) optimize success for every student
through engagement via cutting-edge neuroscience research.

A culturally relevant curriculum speaks to a more inclusive egalitarian
order rather than an exclusive paradigm based on a traditional layered hierarchy—a pecking order that unfairly marginalizes students with linguistic and
cultural differences. There are a number of concrete steps a culturally competent educator can follow to promote educational equity and set an environment for both student scholastic excellence and enhanced social development:

- First, be respectful. Not only students, but also their parents should
  feel understood and appreciated by school personnel.
- Second, ensure the most enriched curricula for all students. Eschew
  tracking (perceived ability grouping), which has historically marginalized children of color and students who do not speak English.
- Third, demonstrate empathy. As part of cultural competency, it is vital
  to understand someone else's point a view, even though it might not
  be yours.
- Fourth, do not judge in haste. Have the forbearance to wait. Understand that school decisions need to be based on solid information and
  cultural knowledge. Moreover, due to identifiable cultural differences,
  academic and social tasks cannot always meet deadlines. Recall, *if* a
  student learns is more important than *when* a student learns.[52]

Correspondingly, the traditional trope of the "melting pot" to portray cultural amalgamation is more than a bit passé for twenty-first-century schools.
Traditionally, the melting pot theory suggested that immigrants from all over
the world could meld into one particular kind of American steel. As we have
seen in part 1 of this book, specific groups viewed as outsiders (e.g., African Americans, Latinxs, and Native Americans) have never fully been fully
integrated into this process. For too often and for too many, the American

classroom has been a place where distinct languages and cultural practices, folkways, and mores were either not welcomed or unambiguously forbidden. It is important to reassert that the twenty-first-century school must adopt what Geneva Gay has termed culturally responsive teaching.[53] The basis for culturally responsive teaching may be found in the emergent principles, policies, and practices based on long-standing research from a wide variety of fields including pedagogy, social history, anthropology, sociology, psychology, applied linguistics, and neurobiology. A culturally competent teacher plays a pivotal role in setting a classroom atmosphere that celebrates diversity as an enhanced learning opportunity. Accordingly, this environment provides that the entire school community actively endorses the self-worth of every student—especially those youngsters who have been traditionally marginalized. The enormity of the task of providing a world-class education for every student cannot be underestimated. Over half of all children in the United States under the age of five are ethnic or linguistic minorities. According to the U.S. Census Bureau, the 2020 Census is projected to find that more than half of the nation's children (those under 18) are part of a minority race or ethnic group. Moreover, this proportion is expected to increase over time. The Bureau projects that, by 2060, only 36 percent of all children will be single-race non-Hispanic white.[54]

To meet the needs of every student, culturally competent educators must remake their standards-based curricula to "look like" the students they are teaching. There are practical steps teachers can take immediately, from filling the classroom walls with posters and thought-provoking quotations from famous figures from all cultural segments reflecting the student population, to planning and implementing a cooperative atmosphere with different cultural perspectives. Django Paris and H. Samy Alim have written about the concept of culturally sustaining pedagogy, a form of teaching in the school that extends and nurtures linguistic and cultural pluralism as part of a positive social transformation. Such a pedagogy can produce curricula made up from "many voices" so that it reflects the students being taught. For example, providing all students with an opportunity to speak and write about their personal feelings, values, and experiences is a building block to a culturally relevant learning model. Likewise, teachers should view a student's linguistic and cultural heritage as an asset, not as a problem. For instance, schools that set up multilingual curricula (where every student learns a second language) can result in learners who attain superior cross-cultural and language skills, a distinct advantage in the multicultural society of today and tomorrow.[55]

Zaretta Hammond has pointed out that diverse classrooms need a proven framework for optimizing student engagement. Culturally responsive instruction has shown promise especially when it draws on cutting-edge neuroscience research. By combining culturally responsive instruction and implementing brain-compatible pedagogy, a powerful force appears to be unleashed in terms of a synergy among the affective, cognitive, and psychomotor domains. The use of brain research to enhance student learning may lead to greater classroom success.[56] Consider the phenomenon of a positive disposition toward learning. Culturally responsive learning environments can be effective if they are properly designed so that students "feel" the need to be engaged. Emotions are known to cause a strong motivating influence on how the environment is perceived.[57] Culturally competent teachers can make a positive difference in the academic development and social growth of a diverse student population if they know how to design an inclusive environment where student motivation (affective domain) triggers both thinking (cognitive domain) and physical activity (psychomotor domain) to achieve desired goals.

Learning, as in any other human activity, is based on choice, a process in which one decides what or what not to do. In other words, a student's emotions affect his or her decisions. Emotions and feelings are a major factor in the interaction between environmental conditions and human decision processes. Once an environment is experienced one's brain then sorts out which neural connections to strengthen and which to prune. The idea is that we are not thinking beings, but feeling beings that think. In other words, there is empirical evidence that emotions, which produce feelings, overlay our thought process. Antonio Damasio notes in neurobiological terms that decisions emanate from what you or I might call the "gut" or the "heart." They are actually an electrochemical process in numerous regions of the brain. A decision can be initially based in our emotions. That choice is then transferred to memory. That memory recalls our feelings with (sometimes too briefly) or without the seat of cognition that we associate with the frontal lobes.[58] Conceptualizing this, teachers should do two things. First, establish a culturally relevant classroom learning environment using students' prior cultural knowledge to build solid analogies and past experiences that link the curricula. Second, teachers need to model by word and action an atmosphere conducive to positive and reassuring sentiments where a student's culture and language is honored and the student feels both at ease and yet challenged.

Neuroscience research indicates that the brain literally grows as we learn.[59] That is, learning increases dendrite quantity. So, culturally competent educators should teach the most enriched curriculum for all and vary their methodological approaches to different students at different points of brain development. Meaning trumps information. Hence, simply teaching "facts" via a traditional textbook is not enough. When teachers value diverse children with distinct cultural knowledge and languages, they make their students' culture and language an integral part of the curricula. As neurobiology has shown, disposition (how one feels) drives cognition (how one thinks). Today's uninterested "at-risk" students can, with the guidance of a culturally competent teacher, open up new neural corridors based on a genuine desire to learn. Again, one's feelings spark our thoughts and actions, demonstrating that the affective domain is fundamental to the learning process. Although traditional approaches to learning stress cognitive aspects, there is little chance that sustained learning will occur without the student's intrinsic motivation.[60]

The central idea is to enhance an environment of educational equity for every student by an ongoing process of building a culturally relevant curriculum where students feel accepted. If teachers are to be successful in setting an atmosphere where students choose to learn, then that environment must in some direct way relate to the cultural and linguistic realities that students experience each day outside the classroom walls. A culturally relevant curriculum speaks to a more accepting egalitarian order as opposed to a fragmented society that is too often separated by race, sexual orientation, class, language, gender, ethnicity, and socioeconomic ranking. The point is not that attention should only be paid to a student's feelings. There is no doubt that the ability to think critically (cognition) and to act (psychomotor) form the basis of the learning process.[61] What an enlightened educator must incorporate into her or his approach is to see that emotions that lead to feelings are primal to the learning process. The spark to learn is triggered by emotions, which lead to student choice. Inspiration is a feeling from within the student. It is imperative that culturally competent teachers set an environment where all students feel the impulse to choose to be inspired, motivated, and ultimately empowered.

Dual Paradigm of Onsite and Online

One aspect of a new dual paradigm to genuinely integrate the American public school combines innovative twenty-first-century online education and related social media to promote a sharing of knowledge via the merging of text and imagery. A second facet of the proposed dual paradigm that focuses on academics in action is service learning. Service learning is community engagement pedagogy. It combines learning goals instruction and reflection with community service to mutually benefit both student growth and the common good.[62] Together, the elements of service learning and online education can provide part of the solution to growing resegregation by bringing students of diverse backgrounds together in a working atmosphere to provide a more inclusive learning environment. By embracing positive social change in education, new models based on quality education via equality in education can help integrate the contemporary American elementary and secondary public school.

By harnessing the forces of twenty-first-century technology and service learning, meaningful community service can be linked to a school's curriculum and a new learning ecology is born. There can be little doubt from an educational and societal basis that the online experience in education in this century has provided new dimensions in terms of time and place for educators and students alike.[63] A familiar narrative in today's educational research is that there has been a perceived shift from a traditional transmission model in onsite education to the possibility of a more learner-centered format found in the online experience. Just as the notions of inclusion and exclusion form dueling philosophical viewpoints in a battle for the soul of American education, the relatively new model of inclusive online education can be seen as an instructional choice offering an abundant array of opportunities. In contrast, the traditional onsite classroom has a history of both exclusivity and scarcity.[64] The traditional model, which enrolls all but a small fraction of over fifty million public school students, for too many and for too long has continued a well-known formula based on finite schedules (e.g., time and place), resulting in a paucity of opportunity. For example, one can easily observe that many traditional public schools have one catalog defining the curricula for all students; one starting time (a specific hour of a specific day and from semester to semester); one place to attend class; and one predetermined faculty member who teaches an assigned class or section of a class in a "brick and mortar" classroom. In addition, the public schools are more segregated today than they were 40 years ago, which inherently limits academic achievement and social growth.[65]

In contrast, although in an emergent stage, online education is quickly evolving. Virtual schools are in practically every corner of the nation. In terms of higher education, the growth of online enrollments in the United States has increased since the turn of the century, "irrespective of an expanding or shrinking economy and rising or declining overall college enrollment."[66] In contrast to the traditional paradigm, the online model features an abundance of opportunity where the defining characteristics have to do with user-friendly variances of time, place, and selection of courses. For instance, typically in the online format one can plainly observe a growing trend that has resulted in tens of thousands of online courses; classes that start every month if not every week; virtual global access to resources; and an abundance of qualified faculty that both teach and mentor diverse groups of students.

Prospects for future development in the American public school can forward a new pedagogic ecology where an inclusive philosophy and practice can take root. Accordingly, this virtual environment can provide an atmosphere where a wide variety of participants from distinct geographical locations feel at liberty to share diverse ideas in order to create community-based knowledge without tight time constraints. The result can be an authentic democratic setting where students are challenged to learn while retaining a sense of well-being and acceptance. In understanding the advantages and disadvantages of distinct methodological approaches, well-informed educators can devise creative platforms and develop networks of online-onsite (hybrid) courses. It has long been known that technology affects the delivery of learning in a profound way.[67] These courses would allow for face-to-face meetings with other students from diverse backgrounds, countering the ever-growing problem of traditional segregated onsite classrooms. In can be argued that the contemporary learner needs nurturing in this new ever-changing educational paradigm that can incorporate the best of both models. Such a hybrid online and onsite format can be based on a philosophical commitment to inclusion and a methodological approach to promote diversity.

Hybrid Model Plus Service Learning

Consider a dual paradigm that incorporates online education and integrated field experiences based on a service learning paradigm.[68] Perhaps this may provide part of the answer to resisting the ever more segregated twenty-first-century classroom. What is called for is a plan where diverse students *work* together toward a common goal. The opportunity for people of many backgrounds to appreciate the efforts of others outside their social network is imperative for quality education in a pluralistic nation. For example, one might convey this idea to the school community in Los Angeles, California— one of the most segregated school districts in one of the most segregated states in the nation.[69] Consider a formal multischool project via service learning and online education to bring students of different races, languages, and ethnicities together in a citywide poetry festival, perhaps cosponsored by the district's board of education and local radio and TV stations. To activate this plan, the use of online education would be pivotal, because online education can provide curricular access to all students at school or in the home. A high school hybrid onsite-online English genre course would deliver an enriched curriculum for all, via a wide variety of methodological approaches in this dual paradigm. Students would learn about different forms of poetry from sonnets to haiku, to *letrilla*, to ballads, to free verse to rap. They would communicate both through online streaming video and threaded discussions to begin to analyze and then write original poetry. The curriculum would follow the appropriate state-mandated English language and bilingual education standards. Poems would be read by all in class and online as a part of authentic assessment. A citywide festival would be planned on a school day where students and community members could meet for artistic recitals. While the poetry festival is a service to the community and standards-based education is taking place, there is the additional benefit of having diverse students *work* together on poetry projects.

Integration is more than geographical proximity. Simply attending the same school or learning location is not sufficient. Proximity does not equal social interaction. When students actually study together, social bonds and cross-cultural understanding can grow.[70] When diverse students work together on a mutual interest, it provides the opportunity to listen, learn, and then express different points of view in a number of multicultural, multilingual, and multiracial settings. In another example, merging service learning with a hybrid online-onsite education can become a reality with inspired innovative lesson planning and school-to-school coordination. For instance, after students have taken an ecology unit in an online diverse classroom and made social media contacts with other learners from many different backgrounds, students from all over the community are physically transported to a local mangrove forests to study the biocomplexity of that location's ecosystem. Observations are made, notes are taken, and reports are written. There

Figure 33. Enlightened schools need to devise strategies to accommodate every student from different parts of the community by providing the kind of enriched educational experience that brings diverse groups of learners together in a working relationship.

is one other thing that happens: students of diverse backgrounds find common ground for discussions and an exchange of ideas and values on a range of issues. This provides opportunities for diverse populations to interact and develop academically while growing socially.

As was noted earlier, service learning proposes to reach out and build bridges to the community by mixing the school's academic curricula with projects that are designed to provide a service that benefits the learner as well as the community. In essence, service learning is both a philosophy of education and an instructional methodology with direct ties to a school's curricula. Philosophically, service learning promotes the idea that education should put a high value on social responsibility in preparing students to live in a democratic society. As a methodological approach, service learning is a blend of service activities stemming from the academic curricula, which allows students to become actively involved in problem solving and organizational and team skills to help them in their future work and learning. In other words, service learning is geared to connect students to diverse communities by actively engaging them in the learning process as they meet human needs.

Figure 34. The mesh of new innovative ways of learning among diverse students may well contribute to learning by building on a wider range of prior knowledge. By gaining and using new information through their online reading and testing, these diverse students then join in a planned field experience that includes in-person observations, experimentations, and reflections.

Correspondingly, service learning can expose learners to diverse groups of people from different backgrounds, ages, and cultures, while making the students aware of community issues rooted in the standards-based curriculum. True service learning requires that both the service providers and the service recipients derive a benefit. Seen from the vantage point of school curricula, service learning contextualizes student academic achievement and social growth.[71] In actuality, human ecology is also being observed and studied. As has been noted, people learn and appreciate each other when they have the opportunity to work together. Again, simple geographical proximity in a class setting does not equal social integration. The very real skills communication and cooperation with others are competencies critical in a pluralistic society.

Today's schools have a choice. Unless a school sets high expectations for all students and provides the critical resources that permit diverse children to perform at a high level, the same old lesson that white children and children of color learn is simply and unfortunately a reinforcement of the traditional racial hierarchies that assume racial inferiority and (white) superiority.[72] Correspondingly, pseudo-scientific notions such as "deficit thinking" theorize that low income minority students' lack of success in school is due to deficiencies (e.g., poor home socialization, absence of motivation, or simply low intelligence) that blunt the leaning process.[73] In short, it is blaming the victim. America's public school teachers and students need a better understanding of the ever more culturally and linguistically diverse communities in which they live. Service learning with a boost via new technologies continues to have untapped potential to actively help students to not only grow academically but develop socially. Thus, as students learn an enriched curriculum they also benefit in the understanding and appreciation of a wide variety of diverse students who make up their community.

Final Thoughts

America's public education has historically provided dual and disparate opportunities and outcomes for its children. From the nineteenth century common school to the twenty-first-century public school there has been a struggle between an inclusionary versus an exclusionary paradigm within American culture. After reviewing the historical and political record there arises a pedagogic imperative for America's school of tomorrow: in order to provide a free public education of the highest quality for every child there must be an unambiguous rejection of today's resegregation. A functioning democracy recommends it, pedagogy requires it, the Constitution demands it.

Where does one start? The answer might well be the biblical proclamation: *In principio erat Verbum*—in the beginning was the word. If discussions about the reality of resegregation—among the public in general, but especially in teacher education programs in particular—do not happen, then life proceeds as if this pernicious truth did not exist. Many times, when an important national problem is neither debated nor even discussed it may be due to ignorance or disinterest. However, in our nation's teacher education programs, housed in the prestigious schools and colleges across the nation, the absence of the discussion of and remedies to counteract growing resegregation is more than unacceptable, it is malpractice. In a segregated system, children are cheated of their birthright in a nation that claims to strive for freedom and justice for all. A free public education that provides an equal opportunity for all children is more than an American ideal, it is the very democratic underpinning upon which all else rests. Historic cracks in that foundation that grow wider each day are due to a system of education that proclaims inclusion, but all too often practices exclusion. There can be no quality education in a democracy without equality in education. New solutions and a willingness to pursue fairness for every child by combating segregation is not just a noble cause, it is the professional responsibility of every educator. The education of fifty million children is at stake.

NOTES

Preface

1. Sarah Mondale and Sarah B. Patton, eds., *School: The Story of American Public Education* (Boston: Beacon Press, 2001), 8.

2. Johann N. Neem, *Democracy's Schools: The Rise of Public Education in America (How Things Worked)* (Baltimore: Johns Hopkins University Press, 2017), chapter 1.

3. James A. Banks, *Cultural Diversity and Education: Foundations, Curriculum and Teaching*, 6th ed. (New York: Routledge, 2015), chapter 3.

4. Neem, *Democracy's Schools*, chapter 1.

5. Mark Ryan, *Ask the Teacher: A Practitioner's Guide to Teaching and Learning in the Diverse Classroom* (Boston: Allyn and Bacon, 2008), 48.

6. Ansley T. Erickson, *Making the Unequal Metropolis: School Desegregation and Its Limits* (Chicago: University of Chicago Press, 2017), 4.

Part 1

1. David Tyack, "Democracy in Education—Who Needs It?," *Editorial Projects in Education* 19, no. 12 (1999): 42.

2. Adlai Stevenson, "Address to the Citizens' School Committee, Chicago, Illinois" (1948), accessed October 15, 2019, http://adlaitoday.org/ideas/quotes_care.html

3. Gary Orfield, Erica Frankenberg, Jongyeon Ee, and Genevieve Siegel-Hawley, *Brown at 62: School Segregation by Race, Poverty, and State* (Los Angeles: UCLA Civil Rights Project/Proyecto Derechos Civiles, 2016), 11. https://www.civilrightsproject.ucla. edu/research/k-12-education/integration-and-diversity/brown-at-62-school-segregation-by-race-poverty-and-state

4. Mark Ryan, *Ask the Teacher: A Practitioner's Guide to Teaching and Learning in the Diverse Classroom* (Boston: Allyn and Bacon, 2008), 316.

5. Jeannie Oakes, *Keeping Track: How Schools Structure Inequality* (New Haven: Yale University Press, 1985), 191.

6. Ryan, *Ask the Teacher*, 10.

7. Nora E. Hyland, "Detracking in Social Studies: A Path to a More Democratic Education?," *Theory into Practice* 45, no. 1 (2006): 64–71.

8. Prudence L Carter, "Education's Limitations and Its Radical Possibilities," *Contexts: Sociology for the Public*, June 18, 2018, https://contexts.org/articles/educations-limitations-and-its-radical-possibilities/

9. John Dewey, *Democracy and Education* (New York: Macmillan Company, 1916), 100–102.

10. Oakes, *Keeping Track*, 15–17.

11. Benjamin Franklin, "Proposals Relating to the Education of Youth in Pennsylvania (October 1749)," *Founders Online*, National Archives, accessed September 29, 2019, https://founders.archives.gov/documents/Franklin/01-03-02-0166

12. Thomas Jefferson to Peter Carr, September 7, 1814, accessed October 15, 2019, https://www.encyclopediavirginia.org/Letter_from_Thomas_Jefferson_to_Peter_Carr_September_7_1814

13. Thomas Jefferson, "Notes on the State of Virginia" (1787), Avalon Project, Yale Law School, http://www.gutenberg.org/files/56313/56313-h/56313-h.htm

14. Ibram X. Kendi, *Stamped from the Beginning: The Definitive History of Racist Ideas in America* (New York: Nation Books, 2016), 9–10.

15. Thomas Jefferson Foundation, "VI. Conclusions: Report of the Research Committee on Thomas Jefferson and Sally Hemings," Thomas Jefferson Foundation: Charlottesville, 2000, https://www.monticello.org/site/plantation-and-slavery/vi-conclusions

16. Thomas Jefferson, "Notes on the State of Virginia, Query XVIII: Manners" (1781), Teaching American History, https://teachingamericanhistory.org/library/document/notes-on-the-state-of-virginia-query-xviii-manners/

17. Kimberly Tolley, "Slavery," in *Miseducation: A History of Ignorance-Making in America and Abroad*, ed. A. J. Angulo (Baltimore: John Hopkins University Press, 2016), 14.

18. Kendi, *Stamped from the Beginning*, 4.

19. Thomas Jefferson to Charles Yancy, January 6, 1816, *Founders Online*, National Archives, accessed October 15, 2019, https://founders.archives.gov/documents/Jefferson/03-09-02-0209

20. Mondale and Patton, *School*, 23.

21. Derrick Darby and John L. Ruby, *The Color of Mind: Why the Origins of the Achievement Gap Matter* (Chicago: University of Chicago Press, 2018), 112.

22. Benjamin Franklin, "A Proposal for Promoting Useful Knowledge, 14 May 1743," *Founders Online*, National Archives, accessed September 29, 2019, https://founders.archives.gov/documents/Franklin/01-02-02-0092

23. Timothy Claxton, *Memoir of a Mechanic* (Boston: George W. Light, 1839), 83.

24. William Maclure, *Opinions on Various Subjects Dedicated to the Industrious Producers* (New Harmony, Ind.: School Press, 1831), 150.

25. Mondale and Patton, *School*, 25–60.

26. Hilary J. Moss, *Schooling Citizens: The Struggle for African American Education in Antebellum America* (Chicago: University of Chicago Press, 2009), 3.

27. Moss, *Schooling Citizens*, 4.

28. Carolyn Eastman, *A Nation of Speechifiers: Making an American Public after the Revolution* (Chicago: University of Chicago Press, 2009), 1–14.

29. Neem, introduction to *Democracy's Schools*; Nancy Beadie, *Education and the Creation of Capital in the Early American Republic* (New York: Cambridge University Press, 2014), 16.

30. John Demos, *The Heathen School: A Story of Hope and Betrayal in the Age of the Early Republic* (New York: Alfred A. Knopf, 2017), 32–37; David Wallace Adams, *Education for Extinction: American Indians and the Boarding School Experience, 1875–1928* (Lawrence: University Press of Kansas, 1995), 335–37.

31. Richard H. Pratt, "The Advantages of Mingling Indians with Whites" (1892), in *Americanizing the American Indians: Writings by the "Friends of the Indian," 1880–1900,* ed. Francis Paul Prucha (Cambridge: Harvard University Press, 1973), 260–71.

32. Catharine Beecher, *Suggestions Respecting Improvements in Education: Presented to the Trustees of the Hartford Female Seminary, and Published at Their Request* (Hartford, Conn.: Packer and Butler, 1829), 7.

33. Kimberly Tolley, introduction to *Heading South to Teach: The World of Susan Nye Hutchison, 1815–1845* (Chapel Hill: University of North Carolina Press, 2015).

34. Tolley, introduction to *Heading South to Teach.*

35. Margaret Nash, *Women's Education in the United States, 1780–1840* (New York: Palgrave Macmillan, 2005), 1–3.

36. Matthew Fegan, "Gender Divide: Re-Examining the Feminization of Teaching in the Nineteenth Century with Emphasis on the Displaced Male Teacher" (2012), senior independent study thesis, paper 3816, https://openworks.wooster.edu/independent-study/3816; 34–35; Marvin C. Alkin, "A History of Teaching in America—as Told by Those Who Know," *Waking Bear,* March 5, 2007, http://www.wakingbear.com/archives/a-history-of-teaching-in-america-as-told-by-those-who-know

37. "Northwest Ordinance, July 13, 1787: An Ordinance for the Governing of the Territory of the United States Northwest of the River Ohio," Avalon Project at Yale University, accessed September 16, 2019, https://avalon.law.yale.edu/18th_century/nworder.asp

38. Oakes, *Keeping Track,* 17.

39. David F. Labaree, *Someone Has to Fail: The Zero-Sum Game of Public Schooling* (Cambridge: Harvard University Press, 2010), 3.

40. Oakes, *Keeping Track,* 18, 23–24.

41. Diane Ravitch, *Left Back: A Century of Battles over School Reforms* (New York: Simon and Schuster, 2001), chapter 1; National Education Association, *Report of the Committee of Ten on Secondary School Studies* (New York: American Book Co., 1894), as found in Nelson Bossing, *Principles of Secondary Education* (New York: Prentice-Hall, 1949), 155.

42. Oakes, *Keeping Track,* 20.

43. Charles Dudley Warner, *The Education of the Negro* (1900), 13, Project Gutenberg, accessed September 19, 2019, http://www.gutenberg.org/dirs/3/1/1/3114/3114.txt

44. Mondale and Patton, *School,* 55–58.

45. Oakes, *Keeping Track,* 20.

46. Warner, *Education of the Negro,* accessed September 19, 2019. http://www.gutenberg.org/dirs/3/1/1/3114/3114.txt

47. Oakes, *Keeping Track,* 21.

48. Mondale and Patton, *School,* 97–104.

49. Mondale and Patton, *School,* 95.

50. "Ellwood Patterson Cubberley," Prabook, accessed October 2, 2019, https://prabook.com/web/ellwood.cubberley/3733140

51. Edward T. James, ed., *The Dictionary of American Biography, Supplement Three: 1941–1945* (New York: Charles Scribner's Sons, 1974), 205–7.

52. Ellwood P. Cubberley, *The History of Education* (Cambridge: Riverside Press, 1920), 833–39.

53. Cubberley, *History of Education*, 833–39.

54. Cubberley, *History of Education*, 494–95.

55. Rudyard Kipling. "White Man's Burden," *Times* (UK), February 4, 1899, http://www.kiplingsociety.co.uk/rg_burden1.htm

56. Cubberley, *History of Education*, 789.

57. William McKinley, as quoted in Brian D'Haeseleer and Roger Peace, "The War of 1898 and the U.S.-Filipino War, 1899–1902," United States Foreign Policy History and Resource Guide, http://peacehistory-usfp.org/1898–1899

58. Cubberley, *History of Education*, 839.

59. Bess Keller, "Stanford Professor Created a New Breed of Professional," *Education Week* 19, no. 12 (1999): 1–4.

60. Cubberley, as quoted in Mondale and Patton, *School*, 98.

61. Ellwood P. Cubberley, *Changing Conceptions of Education in America* (Boston: Houghton, Mifflin, 1909), 15.

62. Ellwood P. Cubberley, *Public School Administration* (Boston: Houghton, Mifflin, 1916), 338.

63. Diane Ravitch, "American Traditions in Education," in *A Primer on America's Schools*, ed. Terry M. Moe (Stanford: Hoover Institution Press, 2001), 3–5.

64. Clarence S. Yoakum and Robert Means Yerkes, eds., *Army Mental Tests* (New York: Henry Holt and Company, 1920), 30.

65. Carl Brigham, *A Study of American Intelligence* (Princeton: Princeton University Press, 1923), 210.

66. Dewey, *Democracy and Education*, 54.

67. Ryan, *Ask the Teacher*, 53.

68. Oakes, *Keeping Track*, 40.

69. David Tyack and Larry Cuban, *Tinkering with Utopia: A Century of Public School Reform*, 6th ed. (Cambridge: Harvard University Press, 2003), 58.

70. Linda Darling-Hammond, "Unequal Opportunity: Race and Education," Brookings, March 1, 1998, https://www.brookings.edu/articles/unequal-opportunity-race-and-education/

71. Andrew R. Highsmith and Ansley T. Erickson, "Segregation as Splitting, Segregation as Joining: Schools, Housing, and the Many Modes of Jim Crow," *American Journal of Education* 121, no. 4 (August 2015): 563–95; Jo Boaler, "Ability and Mathematics: The Mindset Revolution That Is Reshaping Education," https://www.youcubed.org/wp-content/uploads/14_Boaler_FORUM_55_1_web.pdf

72. Ryan, *Ask the Teacher*, 6–8.

73. Labaree, *Someone Has to Fail*, 3.

Part 2

1. Mark Ryan, "The Enduring Legacy: Structured Inequality in America's Public Schools," *Canyon Journal of Interdisciplinary Studies* 5, no. 2 (2016): 66–84.

2. "Trump Judicial Nominees and *Brown v. Board of Education*," *Weekend Edition*, National Public Radio, May 19, 2019, https://www.npr.org/2019/05/19/724747911/trump-judicial-nominees-and-brown-v-board-of-education

3. Donald J. Trump, as quoted in Alan Smith, "Trump Says Congresswomen of Color Should 'Go Back' and Fix the Places They 'Originally Came From,'" *NBC News*, July 14, 2019, https://www.nbcnews.com/politics/donald-trump/trump-says-progressive-con gresswomen-should-go-back-where-they-came-n1029676

4. Russell Contreras, "A History of Racism Is Woven into the US Presidency," Associated Press, July 30, 2019, https://www.apnews.com/b0fe304f1fad44e19e5ff4490ad1110c

5. Erica Frankenberg and Gary Orfield, eds., *The Resegregation of Suburban Schools: A Hidden Crisis in American Schools* (Cambridge: Harvard Educational Press, 2012), 7.

6. Frankenberg and Orfield, *Resegregation of Suburban Schools*, 5–6.

7. *Milliken v. Bradley*, 418 U.S. 717 (1974), accessed October 20, 2019, https://supreme.justia.com/cases/federal/us/418/717/case.html

8. Thurgood Marshall, "*Milliken v. Bradley*/Dissent Marshall," https://en.wikisource.org/wiki/Milliken_v._Bradley/Dissent_Marshall

9. Frankenberg and Orfield, *Resegregation of Suburban Schools*, 5–6; Andrew R. Highsmith, *Demolition Means Progress: Flint, Michigan and the Fate of the American Metropolis* (Chicago: University of Chicago Press, 2015), 5.

10. Nina Totenberg, "Heated Arguments Fly at Supreme Court over Race in College Admissions," *All Things Considered*, National Public Radio, December 9, 2015, http://www.npr.org/2015/12/09/459099492/supreme-court-revisits-affirmative-action-in-high er-education

11. Totenberg, "Heated Arguments."

12. Totenberg, "Heated Arguments."

13. "Trump to Nominate 'Strict Constructionist' to Supreme Court: Pence," Reuters, January 26, 2017, https://www.reuters.com/article/us-usa-court-pence-idUSKBN15A2RR; Debra Cassens Weiss, "Kavanaugh Lands in Top Six in 'Scalia-ness' Ranking of SCOTUS Contenders; Who Is No. 1?," *ABA Journal*, January 16, 2018, http://www.abajournal.com/news/article/kavanaugh_lands_in_top_six_in_scalia_ness_ranking_of_scotus_contenders_who

14. Ryan, "Enduring Legacy," 66–84.

15. Timothy N. Thurber, "Goldwaterism Triumphant? Race and the Republican Party, 1965–1968," *Journal of the Historical Society* 7, no. 3 (September 2007), Wiley Online Library, https://doi.org/10.1111/j.1540–5923.2007.00221.x

16. David J. McCord, ed.. *The Statutes at Large of South Carolina. Vol. 7, Containing the Acts Relating to Charleston, Courts, Slaves, and Rivers* (Columbia, S.C.: A.S. Johnston, 1840), 397.

17. Kevin Phillips, interviewed on *Bill Moyer's Journal*, by Bill Moyers, Public Broadcasting System, November 7, 2008, http://www.pbs.org/moyers/journal/11072008/watch3.html

18. Barack H. Obama, "Remarks by the President at LBJ Presidential Library Civil Rights Summit," April 10, 2014, White House Office of the Press Secretary, https://obamawhitehouse.archives.gov/the-press-office/2014/04/10/remarks-president-lbj-presi dential-library-civil-rights-summit

19. Mark Shields, "The 'Death' of the GOP," Creators Syndicate, July 2, 2016, http://www.creators.com/read/mark-shields/07/16/the-death-of-the-gop

20. Lyndon B. Johnson, "Johnson's Remarks on Signing the Elementary and Secondary Act," speech presented at Johnson City, Texas, April 11, 1965, LBJ Presidential Library, http://www.lbjlibrary.org/lyndon-baines-johnson/timeline/johnsons-remarks-on-sign ing-the-elementary-and-secondary-education-act

21. Daniel Schugurensky, "History of Education: Selected Moments of the Twentieth Century," accessed October 2, 2019, http://schugurensky.faculty.asu.edu/moments/1965elemsec.html

22. Melissa Block, "LBJ Carried Poor Texas Town with Him in Civil Rights Fight," *All Things Considered*, National Public Radio, April 11, 2014, http://www.npr.org/2014/04/11/301820334/lbj-carried-cotulla-with him-in-civil-rights-fight

23. "Separate Is Not Equal: *Brown v. Board of Education*," Smithsonian Institution, accessed October 20, 2019, http://americanhistory.si.edu/brown/history/6-legacy/delib erate-speed.html

24. Mondale and Patton, *School*, 149.

25. Hubert H. Humphrey, "1948 Democratic National Convention Address," speech presented at the 1948 Democratic National Convention, Philadelphia, July 14, 1948, American Rhetoric, http://www.americanrhetoric.com/speeches/huberthumphey 1948dnc.html

26. Hubert H. Humphrey, as quoted in David Frum, *How We Got Here: The '70s* (New York: Basic Books, 2000), 252.

27. Seymour Hersh, *The Price of Power: Kissinger in the Nixon White House* (New York: Summit Books, 1983), 110.

28. William F. Buckley, "Why the South Must Prevail" (1957), accessed October 20, 2019, https://adamgomez.files.wordpress.com/2012/03/whythesouthmustprevail-1957.pdf

29. William A. Rusher, "Crossroads for the GOP," *National Review*, February 12, 1963, accessed September 15, 2012, http://www.unz.org/Pub/NationalRev-1963feb12–00109

30. Kenneth O'Reilly, *Nixon's Piano: Presidents and Racial Politics from Washington to Clinton* (New York: Free Press, 1995), 297.

31. Richard M. Nixon, "President Nixon on School Busing," April 29, 1971, Nixon Foundation, accessed October 20, 2019, https://www.youtube.com/watch?v=7d8Zm9kl488

32. Richard M. Nixon, "Statement about Desegregation of Elementary and Secondary Schools," March 24, 1970, American Presidency Project, https://www.presidency.ucsb.edu/documents/statement-about-desegregation-elementary-and-secondary-schools

33. William H. Chafe, *The Unfinished Journey: America since World War II*, 6th ed. (New York: Oxford University Press, 2007), 368–69; Stephen Ambrose, *Nixon: The Triumph of a Politician, 1962–1972* (New York: Simon and Shuster, 1989), 408.

34. Michael A. Genovese, *The Nixon Presidency: Power and Politics in Turbulent Times* (New York: Praeger, 1990), 85.

35. Richard Rothstein and Mark Santow, "A Different Kind of Choice: Educational Inequality and the Continuing Significance of Racial Segregation," Economic Policy Insti-

tute, August 21, 2012, https://archive.org/stream/ERIC_ED537326/ERIC_ED537326_
djvu.txt

    36. Leon Panetta and Peter Gall, *Bring Us Together: The Nixon Team and the Civil
Rights Retreat* (Philadelphia: J. B. Lippincott, 1971), 197, 222.

    37. David Middlecamp, "Getting Fired by Nixon Turned Out Pretty Well for Leon
Panetta," *Tribune* (San Luis Obispo, CA), May 12, 2017, https://www.sanluisobispo.com/
news/local/news-columns-blogs/photos-from-the-vault/article150282472.html

    38. John A. Farrell, "Nixon's Vietnam Treachery," *New York Times*, December 31,
2016, http://www.nytimes.com/2016/12/31/opinion/sunday/nixons-vietnam-treachery.
html?action=click&pgtype=Homepage&clickSource=story-heading&module=opin-
ion-c-col-left-region&region=opinion-c-col-left-region&WT.nav=opinion-c-col-left-re-
gion&_r=0

    39. Hubert Humphrey, as quoted in Carl Solberg, *Hubert Humphrey: A Biography* (St.
Paul: Minnesota Historical Society Press, 2003), 430.

    40. Lawrence J. McAndrews, "Missing the Bus: Gerald Ford and School Desegrega-
tion," *Presidential Studies Quarterly* 99, no. 4 (1997): 791–804.

    41. Gerald Ford, "Interview on CBS' *Face the Nation*, by George Herman, CBS News, June
6, 1976, https://www.presidency.ucsb.edu/documents/interview-cbs-news-face-the-nation

    42. Nate Silver, "GOP Has Always Been Dominated by White Voters," FiveThirtyEight,
July 1, 2009, http://fivethirtyeight.com/features/gop-has-always-been-dominated-by-
white/

    43. Christopher Lydon, "Carter Defends All-White Areas," *New York Times*, April 7,
1976, http://www.nytimes.com/1976/04/07/archives/carter-defends-allwhite-areas-says-
government-shouldnt-try-to-end.html?_r=0

    44. Jimmy Carter, as quoted in Myungsung Kim, "Afrofuturism, Science Fiction, and
the Reinvention of African American Culture" (PhD diss., Arizona State University, 2017),
145. https://repository.asu.edu/attachments/189587/content/Kim_asu_0010E_17187.pdf

    45. Thomas Stephen Neuberger and Thomas C. Crumplar, "Tax-Exempt Religious
Schools under Attack: Conflicting Goals of Religious Freedom and Racial Integration," 49
Fordham Law Review 229 (1980), http://ir.lawnet.fordham.edu/flr/vol49/iss3/1

    46. Tim Neftali, "Ronald Reagan's Long Hidden Racist Conversation with Richard
Nixon," *Atlantic*, July 30, 2019, https://www.theatlantic.com/ideas/archive/2019/07/ron
ald-reagans-racist-conversation-richard-nixon/595102/

    47. "*Bob Jones University v. the United States*," Cornell University Law School: Legal
Information Institute, accessed October 20, 2019, https://www.law.cornell.edu/supreme
court/text/461/574

    48. Bernard Weinraub, "Burger Retiring, Rehnquist Named Chief; Scalia, Appeals
Judge, Chosen for Court," *New York Times*, June 18, 1986, https://www.nytimes.
com/1986/06/18/us/burger-retiring-rehnquist-named-chief-scalia-appeals-judge-chosen-
for-court.html

    49. Ronald Reagan, as quoted by Juan Williams, "Reagan Blames Courts for Education
Decline," *Washington Post*, June 30, 1983, https://www.washingtonpost.com/archive/
politics/1983/06/30/reagan-blames-courts-for-education-decline/729b84ac-d6de-4abb-
b628-21d6b6b4e872/

50. Drew S. Days III, "Turning Back the Clock: The Reagan Administration and Civil Rights," *Harvard Civil Rights–Civil Liberties Law Review* 19, no. 309 (1984): 318–24.

51. Barbara M. Lane, "Construction of the Racist Republican" (PhD thesis, Georgia State University, 2014), 59. https://scholarworks.gsu.edu/history_theses/81

52. Juan Williams, "Reagan, the South, and Civil Rights," *Politically Speaking*, National Public Radio, June 10, 2004, http://www.npr.org/templates/story/story.php?sto ryId=1953700; Terry Drinkwater, "Early Busing Controversy in Southern California," *CBS Evening News*, September 14, 1970, https://www.youtube.com/watch?v=wra-krMEvlU

53. Nikole Hanna-Jones, "School Districts Still Face Fights—and Confusion—on Integration," *Atlantic*, May 2, 2014, http://www.theatlantic.com/education/archive/2014/05/lack-of-order-the-erosion-of-a-once-great-force-for-integration/361563

54. Bob Herbert, "Impossible, Ridiculous, Repugnant," *New York Times*, October 6, 2005, https://www.nytimes.com/2005/10/06/opinion/impossible-ridiculous-repugnant.html

55. Daryl Michael Scott, *Contempt and Pity: Social Policy and the Image of the Damaged Black Psyche, 1880–1996* (Chapel Hill: University of North Carolina Press, 1997), 1–2.

56. Lee Atwater, as quoted in Alexander P. Lamis, *The Two Party South* (Oxford: Oxford University Press, 1990), 267.

57. Lawrence J. McAndrews, "Not the Bus, but Us: George W. Bush and School Desegregation," *Education Foundations* (Winter–Spring 2009): 79, http://files.eric.ed.gov/fulltext/EJ869701.pdf

58. Lawrence J. McAndrews, "Talking the Talk: Bill Clinton and School Desegregation," *International Social Science Review*, September 22, 2004, https://www.thefreelibrary.com/Talking+the+talk%3A+Bill+Clinton+and+school+desegregation.-a0128168183; William. J. Clinton, *Central High School Desegregation Anniversary* C-Span (Little Rock Arkansas, September 25, 1997), video, 56 min., https://www.c-span.org/video/?91570–1

59. James Carney, "Mend It, Don't End It," *Time*, June 24, 2001, http://content.time.com/time/magazine/article/0,9171,134503,00.html

60. William J. Clinton, "A Dialogue on Race with President Bill Clinton," interviewed by Jim Lehrer et al., *Newshour with Jim Lehrer*, PBS News, July 9, 1998, https://www.youtube.com/watch?v=kwlEIPfb_Wo

61. Clinton, "Central High School Desegregation Anniversary."

62. Hillary Clinton, as quoted in Alyson Klein, "What Have the Presidential Candidates Said about School Integration?," *Education Week*, October 31, 2016, http://blogs.edweek.org/edweek/campaign-k-12/2016/10/what_have_the_presidential_can.html

63. McAndrews, "Not the Bus," 70–80.

64. Erwin Chemerinsky, "The Segregation and Resegregation of American Public Education: The Court's Role," *North Carolina Law Review* 81, no. 4 (2003): 1602–05.

65. McAndrews, "Not the Bus,"70.

66. Government Accountability Office, *K-12 Education: Better Use of Information Could Help Agencies Identify Disparities and Address Racial Discrimination* (Washington, D.C.: Government Accountability Office, 2016), accessed October 20, 2019, http://www.gao.gov/assets/680/676745.pdf

67. Alyson Klein, "How Workable Is Trump's $20 Billion School Choice Proposal?," *Education Week*, November 17, 2016, http://blogs.edweek.org/edweek/campaign-k-12/2016/11/trump_20_billion_school_choice_plan.html

68. Fredrik O. Andersson and Michael Ford, "Entry Barriers and Nonprofit Founding Rates: An Examination of the Milwaukee Voucher School Population," *Nonprofit Policy Forum* 8, no. 1: 71–90, accessed November 4, 2019, doi:10.1515/npf-2016–002; Mark Dynarski, "On Negative Effects of Vouchers," Brookings, May 26, 2016, https://www.brookings.edu/research/on-negative-effects-of-vouchers/

69. Emma Brown, "The Overwhelming Whiteness of U.S. Private Schools, in Six Maps and Charts," *Washington Post*, March 29, 2016, https://www.washingtonpost.com/news/education/wp/2016/03/29/the-overwhelming-whiteness-of-u-s-private-schools-in-six-maps-and-charts/?utm_term=.522f4eee2cf8

70. Dana Goldstein, "Obama Education Rules Are Swept Aside by Congress," *New York Times*, March 9, 2017, https://www.nytimes.com/2017/03/09/us/every-student-succeeds-act-essa-congress.html?_r=0

71. Donald J. Trump, "Remarks by President Trump in Joint Address to Congress," White House Press Office, February 28, 2017, https://www.whitehouse.gov/briefings-statements/remarks-president-trump-joint-address-congress/

72. Iris C. Rotberg, "Backtalk: The Social Costs of Proliferating Charter Schools," *Phi Delta Kappan* 100, no. 7 (2019): 80.

73. Catharine Zhang, "The State of Integration in the United States," *Harvard Political Review*, September 9, 2016, http://harvardpolitics.com/united-states/state-integration-united-states/

74. *Parents Involved in Community Schools v. Seattle School District No. 1*, Oyez, accessed October 20, 2019, https://www.oyez.org/cases/2006/05–908

75. Richard Rothstein, "The Racial Achievement Gap, Segregated Schools, and Segregated Neighborhoods—a Constitutional Insult," Economic Policy Institute, November 12, 2014, https://www.epi.org/publication/the-racial-achievement-gap-segregated-schools-and-segregated-neighborhoods-a-constitutional-insult/

76. Rothstein, "Racial Achievement Gap."

77. Paul Douglass, as quoted in Molly Metzger and Henry Webber, *Facing Segregation: Housing Policy Solutions for a Stronger Society* (Oxford: Oxford University Press, 2018), 19.

78. *Parents Involved in Community Schools v. Seattle School District No. 1*, https://www.oyez.org/cases/2006/05–908

79. *Parents Involved in Community Schools v. Seattle School District No. 1*.

80. Rothstein, "Racial Achievement Gap," November 12, 2014, https://www.epi.org/publication/the-racial-achievement-gap-segregated-schools-and-segregated-neighborhoods-a-constitutional-insult/

81. Arnold R. Hirsch, *Making the Second Ghetto: Race and Housing in Chicago, 1940–1960* (Chicago: University of Chicago Press, 1983), 14.

82. Rothstein, "Racial Achievement Gap," November 12, 2014, https://www.epi.org/publication/the-racial-achievement-gap-segregated-schools-and-segregated-neighborhoods-a-constitutional-insult/

Part 3

1. Hanna-Jones, "School Districts Still Face Fights—and Confusion—on Integration."

2. Frankenberg and Orfield, *Resegregation of Suburban Schools*, 5–6.

3. Jessica Trounstine, *Segregation by Design: Local Politics and Inequality in American Cities* (Cambridge: Cambridge University Press, 2018), 2–3.

4. Erickson, *Making the Unequal Metropolis*, 4.

5. Jennifer Ayscue and Erica Frankenberg, "Desegregation and Integration," *Oxford Bibliographies*, February 25, 2016, http://www.oxfordbibliographies.com/view/document/obo-9780199756810/obo-9780199756810–0139.xml

6. Highsmith and Erickson, "Segregation as Splitting, Segregation as Joining.

7. Katie Nodjimbadem, "The Racial Segregation of American Cities Was Anything but Accidental: A Housing Policy Expert Explains How Federal Government Policies Created the Suburbs and the Inner City," *Smithsonian*, May 30, 2017, https://www.smithsonianmag.com/history/how-federal-government-intentionally-racially-segregated-american-cities-180963494/

8. Richard Rothstein, *The Color of Law: A Forgotten History of How Our Government Segregated America*, (Brown University, January 24, 2019), video, 49 min., https://www.youtube.com/watch?v=r9UqnQC7jY4

9. Skylar Olsen, "Black and White Homeownership Rate Gap Has Widened since 1900," Zillow, April 10, 2018, https://www.zillow.com/research/homeownership-gap-widens-19384/

10. Pam Bailey, "How Racism Costs Black Families Hundreds of Billions in Housing Wealth," *Non-Profit Quarterly*, December 4, 2018, https://nonprofitquarterly.org/how-racism-costs-black-families-hundreds-of-billions-in-housing-wealth/

11. Trounstine, *Segregation by Design*, 1–3.

12. "Segregated Neighborhoods, Segregated Schools?," Urban Institute, November 28, 2018, https://www.urban.org/features/segregated-neighborhoods-segregated-schools

13. Michael Hansen, Elizabeth Mann Levesque, Diana Quintero, and Jon Valant, "Have We Made Progress on Achievement Gaps? Looking at Evidence from the New NAEP Results," Brookings, April 17, 2018, https://www.brookings.edu/blog/brown-center-chalkboard/2018/04/17/have-we-made-progress-on-achievement-gaps-looking-at-evidence-from-the-new-naep-results/

14. Sean F. Reardon, Demetra Kalogrides, and Kenneth Shores, "The Geography of Racial/Ethnic Test Score Gaps," *American Journal of Sociology* 124, no. 4 (January 2019): 1164–1221, accessed October 20, 2019, https://www.journals.uchicago.edu/doi/abs/10.1086/700678

15. George Theoharis, "'Forced Busing' Didn't Fail: Desegregation Is the Best Way to Improve Our Schools," *Washington Post*, October 23, 2015, https://www.washingtonpost.com/posteverything/wp/2015/10/23/forced-busing-didnt-fail-desegregation-is-the-best-way-to-improve-our-schools/?utm_term=.32c4caf44d00

16. Darby and Rury, *Color of Mind*, 142.

17. Orfield et al., *Brown at 60*

18. Orfield et al., *Brown at 62*, 5

19. Mondale and Patton, *School*, 149.

20. Amy Stuart Wells, Lauren Fox, and Diana Cordova-Cobo, "How Racially Diverse Schools and Classrooms Can Benefit All Students," Century Foundation, February 9, 2016, https://tcf.org/content/report/how-racially-diverse-schools-and-classrooms-can-benefit-all-students/

21. Wells, Fox, and Cordova-Cobo, "How Racially Diverse Schools and Classrooms Can Benefit All Students."

22. Amy Stuart Wells, Jennifer Holme, Anita T. Revilla, and Awo K. Atanda, *How Desegregation Changed Us: The Effects of Racially Mixed Schools on Students and Society, a Study of Desegregated High Schools and Their Class of 1980 Graduates* (New York: Teachers College, Columbia University, 2004), 6, https://www.tc.columbia.edu/faculty/asw86/faculty-profile/files/ASWells041504.pdf

23. Rucker C. Johnson, *Long-Run Impacts of School Desegregation and School Quality on Adult Attainments*, NBER Working Paper No. 16664, January 2011, revised August 2015 (Cambridge: National Bureau of Economic Research, 2015), unpaged abstract found at https://www.nber.org/papers/w16664.pdf

24. Wells et al., *How Desegregation Changed Us*

25. Aprile D. Benner and Robert Crosnoe, "The Racial/Ethnic Composition of Elementary Schools and Young Children's Academic and Socioemotional Functioning," *American Educational Research Journal* 48, no. 3 (2011): 621–46.

26. Gary Orfield, "Schools More Separate: Consequences of a Decade of Resegregation," Civil Rights Project (Cambridge: Harvard University, 2001), https://eric.ed.gov/?id=ED459217

27. Sean F. Reardon, "School Segregation and Racial Academic Achievement Gaps," paper prepared for "The Coleman Report at Fifty: Its Legacy and Enduring Value," a Russell Sage Foundation conference, April 2016, http://blogs.edweek.org/edweek/inside-school-research/reardon%20segregation%20and%20achievement%20gaps%20apr2016.pdf

28. Ann Mantil, Anne G. Perkins, and Stephanie Aberger, "The Challenge of High-Poverty Schools: How Feasible Is Socioeconomic School Integration?," in *The Future of School Integration*, ed. Richard D. Kahlenberg (New York: Century Foundation, 2012), 155–222.

29. Reardon, "School Segregation and Racial Academic Achievement Gaps," http://blogs.edweek.org/edweek/inside-school-research/reardon%20segregation%20and%20achievement%20gaps%20apr2016.pdf

30. Reardon, Kalogrides, and Shores, "Geography of Racial/Ethnic Test Score Gaps," 1164–1221.

31. Ryan, *Ask the Teacher*, 78–79.

32. Contreras, "History of Racism Is Woven into the US Presidency."

33. Wells et al., *How Desegregation Changed Us*, 5.

34. Wells et al., *How Desegregation Changed Us*, 6.

35. Vivien Stewart, "A Classroom as Wide as the World," in *Curriculum 21: Essential Education for a Changing World*, ed. H. H. Jacobs (Alexandria, Va.: ASCD, 2010), 97–114.

36. Rothstein, "Racial Achievement Gap."

37. Dedrick Asante-Muhammad and Sabrina Terry, "Martin Luther King's Dream

Requires We Overcome 'Our Fantasy Self-Deception,'" *Salon*, January 21, 2019, https://www.salon.com/2019/01/21/martin-luther-kings-dream-requires-we-overcome-our-fantasy-of-self-deception/

38. Orfield et al., *Brown at 62*, 6–9.

39. Rothstein, "Racial Achievement Gap."

40. Jonathan Kozol, Beverly Daniel Tatum, Susan Eaton, and Patricia Gándara, "Resegregation: What's the Answer?," *Educational Leadership* 68, no. 3 (2010): 28–31, accessed October 20, 2019, http://www.ascd.org/publications/educational-leadership/nov10/vol68/num03/Resegregation@-What's-the-Answer%C2%A2.aspx

41. Labaree, *Someone Has to Fail*, 2–3.

42. Kozol et al., "Resegregation."

43. Brian P, Gill, "Charter Schools and Segregation, What the Research Says," EducationNext, November 19, 2018, https://www.educationnext.org/charter-schools-segregation-what-research-says/

44. Frankenberg and Orfield, *Resegregation of Suburban Schools*, 6; Trounstine, introduction to *Segregation by Design*.

45. Kozol et al., "Resegregation."

46. "EDUC 303S: De/Re/Segregation in Education: A Case of Back to the Future?," Duke University, accessed October 20, 2019, https://www.coursicle.com/duke/courses/EDUC/303S/

47. ED/SO 240, "Courses," Bates College: Education, accessed October 20, 2019, http://www.bates.edu/education/academics/courses/

48. "EDU 216: Education Policy and Practice," Cornell College, accessed October 20, 2019. http://catalog.cornellcollege.edu/preview_course_nopop.php?catoid=1&coid=460

49. Fegan, "Gender Divide" https://openworks.wooster.edu/independentstudy/3816; Liana Loewus, "The Nation's Teaching Force Is Still Mostly White and Female," *Education Week*, August 15, 2017, https://www.edweek.org/ew/articles/2017/08/15/the-nations-teaching-force-is-still-mostly.html; Alkin, "History of Teaching in America."

50. Asaf Orr and Joel Baum, *Schools in Transition: A Guide for Supporting Transgender Students in K-12 Schools* (Washington, D.C.: Human Rights Campaign Foundation, 2015), https://www.genderspectrum.org/staging/wp-content/uploads/2015/08/Schools-in-Transition-2015.pdf

51. Tyrone C. Howard, *Why Race and Culture Matter in Schools: Closing the Achievement Gap in America's Classrooms* (New York: Teachers College Press, 2010), 51.

52. Ryan, *Ask the Teacher*, 45.

53. Geneva Gay, *Culturally Responsive Teaching: Theory, Research, and Practice* (New York: Teachers College Press, 2018), preface and chapter 2.

54. U.S. Census Bureau, "New Census Bureau Report Analyzes U.S. Population Projections," News Release, March 3, 2015, U.S. Census Bureau, https://www.census.gov/newsroom/press-releases/2015/cb15-tps16.html

55. Django Paris and H. Samy Alim, eds., *Culturally Sustaining Pedagogies: Teaching and Learning for Justice in a Changing World* (New York: Teachers College Press, 2017), 1–24.

56. Zaretta Hammond, *Culturally Responsive Teaching and the Brain: Promoting*

Authentic Engagement and Rigor among Culturally and Linguistically Diverse Students (Thousand Oaks, Calif.: Corwin, 2015) 3–5; Ryan, *Ask the Teacher*, 78–79.

57. Jonathan Zadra and Gerald Clore, "Emotion and Perception: The Role of Affective Information," *Wiley Interdisciplinary Reviews of Cognitive Science* 2, no. 6 (November–December 2001), https://www.ncbi.nlm.nih.gov/pmc/articles/PMC3203022/

58. Antonio Damasio, *The Strange Order of Things: Life, Feelings, and the Making of Cultures* (New York: Pantheon Books, 2019), 1–3.

59. Ryan, *Ask the Teacher*, 75–77.

60. Ryan, *Ask the Teacher*, 79.

61. Jason Pontin, "The Importance of Feelings," *MIT Technology Review*, June 17, 2014, https://www.technologyreview.com/s/528151/the-importance-of-feelings/

62. Joe Bandy, "What Is Service Learning or Community Engagement?," Vanderbilt University Center for Teaching, accessed October 20, 2019, https://cft.vanderbilt.edu/guides-sub-pages/teaching-through-community-engagement/

63. Andy Tix, "Improving the Experience of Online Education," *Psychology Today*, November 28, 2016, https://www.psychologytoday.com/us/blog/the-pursuit-peace/201611/improving-the-experience-online-education

64. Peter Smith, "From Scarcity to Abundance: IT's Role in Achieving Quality-Assured Mass Higher Education," *Journal of Asynchronous Learning Networks* 15, no. 2 (Spring 2011): 8–12, https://files.eric.ed.gov/fulltext/EJ935573.pdf

65. Smith, "From Scarcity to Abundance."

66. Shailendra Palvia, Prageet Aeron, Paul Gupta, Diptiranjan Mahapatra, Parida Ratri, Rebecca Rosner, and Sumita Sindhi, "Online Education: Worldwide Status, Challenges, Trends, and Implications," *Journal of Global Information Technology Management* 21, no. 4 (2018): 233–41, doi: 10.1080/1097198X.2018.1542262.

67. Daniel L. DeNeui and Tiffany L. Dodge, "Asynchronous Learning Networks and Student Outcomes: The Utility of Online Learning Components in Hybrid Courses," *Journal of Instructional Psychology* 33, no. 4 (2006), http://www.tiffanylorene.com/ALN.pdf

68. Aref Hervani, Marilyn Helms, Raina Rutti, Joanne LaBonte, and Sy Sarkarat, "Service Learning Projects in Online Courses: Delivery Strategies," *Journal of Learning in Higher Education* 11, no. 1 (2015), https://files.eric.ed.gov/fulltext/EJ1141925.pdf

69. Seema Mehta and Michael Finnegan, "Segregation Has Soared in America's Schools as Federal Leaders Largely Looked Away," *Los Angeles Times*, July 8, 2019, https://www.latimes.com/politics/la-na-pol-2020-school-segregation-busing-harris-biden-20190708-story.html; Erica Frankenberg, Jongyeon Ee, Jennifer B. Ayscue, and Gary Orfield, *Harming Our Common Future: America's Segregated Schools 65 Years after Brown* (Los Angeles: UCLA Civil Rights Project, 2019), 25–31, accessed October 20, 2019, https://www.civilrightsproject.ucla.edu/research/k-12-education/integration-and-diversity/harming-our-common-future-americas-segregated-schools-65-years-after-brown/Brown-65–050919v4-final.pdf

70. Ryan, *Ask the Teacher*, 10.

71. Ryan, *Ask the Teacher*, 239–41.

72. Kozol et al., "Resegregation?"

73. Richard Valencia, ed., *The Evolution of Deficit Thinking: Educational Thought and Practice* (London: RoutledgeFalmer, 1997), 1–10.

BIBLIOGRAPHY

Adams, David Wallace. *Education for Extinction: American Indians and the Boarding School Experience, 1875–1928.* Lawrence: University Press of Kansas, 1995.

Alkin, Marvin C. "A History of Teaching in America—as Told by Those Who Know." *Waking Bear,* March 5, 2007. http://www.wakingbear.com/archives/a-history-of-teaching-in-america-as-told-by-those-who-know

Ambrose, Stephen. *Nixon: The Triumph of a Politician, 1962–1972.* New York: Simon and Shuster, 1989.

Andersson, Fredrik O., and Michael Ford. "Entry Barriers and Nonprofit Founding Rates: An Examination of the Milwaukee Voucher School Population." *Nonprofit Policy Forum* 8, no. 1 (January 2017): 71–90. Accessed November 4, 2019, doi:10.1515/npf-2016–002.

Angulo, A. J., ed. *Miseducation: A History of Ignorance-Making in America and Abroad.* Baltimore: Johns Hopkins University Press, 2016.

"The-Anti-Busing-Game." *Washington Post,* July 5, 1977. https://www.washingtonpost.com/archive/politics/1977/07/05/the-anti-busing-game/ea3688be-066a-4d4a-b317–5dba1917ccbd/

Asante-Muhammad, Dedrick, and Sabrina Terry. "Martin Luther King's Dream Requires We Overcome 'Our Fantasy Self-Deception." *Salon,* January 21, 2019. https://www.salon.com/2019/01/21/martin-luther-kings-dream-requires-we-overcome-our-fantasy-of-self-deception/

Ayscue, Jennifer, and Erica Frankenberg. "Desegregation and Integration." *Oxford Bibliographies.* February 25, 2016. http://www.oxfordbibliographies.com/view/document/obo-9780199756810/obo-9780199756810–0139.xml

Bailey, Pam. "How Racism Costs Black Families Hundreds of Billions in Housing Wealth." *Non-Profit Quarterly,* December 4, 2018. https://nonprofitquarterly.org/how-racism-costs-black-families-hundreds-of-billions-in-housing-wealth/

Bandy, Joe. "What Is Service Learning or Community Engagement?" Vanderbilt University Center for Teaching. Accessed October 20, 2019. https://cft.vanderbilt.edu/guides-sub-pages/teaching-through-community-engagement/

Banks, James A. *Cultural Diversity and Education: Foundations, Curriculum and Teaching.* 6th ed. New York: Routledge, 2015.

Beadie, Nancy. *Education and the Creation of Capital in the Early American Republic.* New York: Cambridge University Press, 2014.

Beecher, Catharine. *Suggestions Respecting Improvements in Education: Presented to the Trustees of the Hartford Female Seminary, and Published at their Request.* Hartford: Packer & Butler, 1829.

"The Benefits of Socioeconomically and Racially Integrated Schools and Classrooms." Century Foundation, April, 29, 2019. https://tcf.org/content/facts/the-benefits-of-socioeconomically-and-racially-integrated-schools-and-classrooms/

Benner, Aprile D., and Robert Crosnoe. "The Racial/Ethnic Composition of Ele-
    mentary Schools and Young Children's Academic and Socioemotional Func-
    tioning." *American Educational Research Journal* 48, no. 3 (June 2011): 621–46.
    doi:10.3102/0002831210384838.
Billings, Warren M. "The Law of Servants and Slaves in Seventeenth-Century Virginia."
    Virginia Magazine of History and Biography 99, no. 1 (1991): 45–62.
Block, Melissa. "LBJ Carried Poor Texas Town with Him in Civil Rights Fight."
    All Things Considered, National Public Radio, April 11, 2014. http://www.npr.
    org/2014/04/11/301820334/lbj-carried-cotulla-with him-in-civil-rights-fight
Boaler, Jo. "Ability and Mathematics: The Mindset Revolution That Is Reshaping Edu-
    cation." *Forum* 55, no. 1 (2013): 143–52. Accessed October 20, 2019. https://www.
    youcubed.org/wp-content/uploads/14_Boaler_FORUM_55_1_web.pdf
Board of Education of Oklahoma City Public Schools v. Dowell. Oyez. Accessed October
    20, 2019. https://www.oyez.org/cases/1990/89–1080
Bob Jones University v. the United States. Cornell University Law School: Legal Informa-
    tion Institute. Accessed October 20, 2019. https://www.law.cornell.edu/supreme-
    court/text/461/574
Bossing, Nelson. *Principles of Secondary Education.* New York: Prentice-Hall, 1949.
Brigham, Carl. *A Study of American Intelligence.* Princeton: Princeton University Press,
    1923.
Brown, Emma. "The Overwhelming Whiteness of U.S. Private Schools, in Six Maps and
    Charts." *Washington Post*, March 29, 2016. https://www.washingtonpost.com/news/
    education/wp/2016/03/29/the-overwhelming-whiteness-of-u-s-private-schools-in-
    six-maps-and-charts/?utm_term=.522f4eee2cf8
Brown, Emma. "Trump Picks Billionaire Betsy DeVos, School Voucher Advocate, as Edu-
    cation Secretary." *Washington Post,* November 23, 2016. https://www.washing
    tonpost.com/local/education/trump-picks-billionaire-betsy-devos-school-vouch
    er-advocate-as-education-secretary/2016/11/23/c3d66b94-af96–11e6–840f-e3ebab
    6bcdd3_story.html
Buckley, William F. "Why the South Must Prevail." 1957. Accessed October 20, 2019.
    https://adamgomez.files.wordpress.com/2012/03/whythesouthmustprevail-1957.pdf
Carney, James. "Mend It, Don't End It." *Time*, June 24, 2001. http://content.time.com/
    time/magazine/article/0,9171,134503,00.html
Carter, Prudence L. "Education's Limitations and Its Radical Possibilities." *Contexts:
    Sociology for the Public*, June 18, 2018. https://contexts.org/articles/educations-lim
    itations-and-its-radical-possibilities/
Carter, Prudence L. *Stubborn Roots: Race, Class and Inequality in U.S. and South African
    Schools.* Oxford: Oxford University Press, 2012.
Chemerinsky, Erwin. "The Segregation and Resegregation of American Public Education:
    The Court's Role." *North Carolina Law Review* 81, no. 4 (2003): 1597–1622.
Church, Robert. *Education in the United States, an Interpretive History.* New York: Free
    Press, 1976.
Claxton, Timothy. *Memoir of a Mechanic.* Boston: George W. Light, 1839.
Clinton, William. J. *Central High School Desegregation Anniversary.* C-Span, Septem-

ber 25, 1997. Little Rock, Arkansas. Video, 56 minutes. https://www.c-span.org/
video/?91570–1

Clinton, William J. "A Dialogue on Race with President Bill Clinton." Interviewed by Jim
Lehrer et al., *Newshour with Jim Lehrer*. PBS News, July 9, 1998. https://www.you-
tube.com/watch?v=kwlEIPfb_Wo

Contreras, Russell. "A History of Racism Is Woven into the US Presidency." Associated
Press, July 30, 2019. https://www.apnews.com/b0fe304f1fad44e19e5ff4490ad1l10c.

"Courses." Bates College: Education. Accessed October 20, 2019. http://www.bates.edu/
education/academics/courses/

Cubberley, Ellwood P. *Changing Conceptions of Education in America.* Boston: Houghton,
Mifflin, 1909.

Cubberley, Ellwood, P. *The History of Education.* Cambridge, MA: Riverside Press, 1920.

Cubberley, Ellwood, P. *A Brief History of Education.* Cambridge, MA Riverside Press,
1922.Daley, David. *Ratf**ked: The True Story behind the Secret Plan to Steal America's
Democracy.* New York: Liveright Publishing Company, 2016.

Darby, Derrick, and John L. Ruby. *The Color of Mind: Why the Origins of the Achievement
Gap Matter.* Chicago: University of Chicago Press, 2018.

Darling-Hammond, Linda. "Unequal Opportunity: Race and Education." Brookings, March
1, 1998. https://www.brookings.edu/articles/unequal-opportunity-race-and-education/

Damasio, Antonio. *The Strange Order of Things: Life, Feelings, and the Making of Cultures.*
New York: Pantheon Books, 2019.

Danns, Dionne. *Desegregating Chicago's Public Schools: Policy Implementation, Politics,
and Protest, 1965–1985.* New York: Palgrave Macmillan, 2014.

Davies, Gareth. "Richard Nixon and the Desegregation of Southern Schools." *Journal of
Policy History* 19, no. 4 (2007): 367–94. doi:10.1353/jph.2008.0003.

Days, Drew S., III. "*Turning Back the Clock:* The Reagan Administration and Civil Rights."
Harvard Civil Rights–Civil Liberties Law Review 19, no. 309 (1984): 318–24.

Demos, John. *The Heathen School: A Story of Hope and Betrayal in the Age of the Early
Republic.* New York: Alfred A. Knopf, 2017.

DeNeui, Daniel L., and Tiffany L. Dodge. "Asynchronous Learning Networks and Student
Outcomes: The Utility of Online Learning Components in Hybrid Courses." *Journal
of Instructional Psychology* 33, no. 4 (2006). http://www.tiffanylorene.com/ALN.pdf

Dewey, John. *Democracy and Education.* New York: Macmillan Company, 1916.

Dexter, Elizabeth Anthony. *Colonial Women of Affairs: A Study of Women in Business and
the Professions before 1776.* Boston: Houghton Mifflin, 1931.

D'Haeselee, Brian, and Roger Peace. "The War of 1898 and the U.S.-Filipino War, 1899–
1902." United States Foreign Policy History and Resource Guide. http://peacehisto
ry-usfp.org/1898–1899

Downey, Matthew. *Carl Campbell Brigham: Scientist and Educator.* Princeton: Educational Testing Service, 1961.

Drinkwater, Terry. "Early Busing Controversy in Southern California." *CBS Evening News,*
September 14, 1970. https://www.youtube.com/watch?v=wra-krMEvlU

Dynarski, Mark "On Negative Effects of Vouchers." Brookings, May 26, 2016. https://
www.brookings.edu/research/on-negative-effects-of-vouchers/

Eastman, Carolyn. *A Nation of Speechifiers: Making an American Public after the Revolution*. Chicago: University of Chicago Press, 2009.

"EDU 216: Education Policy and Practice." Cornell College. Accessed October 20, 2019. http://catalog.cornellcollege.edu/preview_course_nopop.php?catoid=1&coid=460

"EDUC 303S: De/Re/Segregation in Education: A Case of Back to the Future?" Duke University. Accessed October 20, 2019. https://www.coursicle.com/duke/courses/EDUC/303S/

"Ellwood Patterson Cubberley." Prabook. Accessed October 2, 2019. https://prabook.com/web/ellwood.cubberley/3733140

Erickson, Ansley T. *Making the Unequal Metropolis: School Desegregation and Its Limits*. Chicago: University of Chicago Press, 2017.

Farrell, John A. "Nixon's Vietnam Treachery." *New York Times*, December 31, 2016. http://www.nytimes.com/2016/12/31/opinion/sunday/nixons-vietnam-treachery.html?action=click&pgtype=Homepage&clickSource=story-heading&module=opinion-c-col-left-region&region=opinion-c-col-left-region&WT.nav=opinion-c-col-left-region&_r=0

Fegan, Matthew, "Gender Divide: Re-Examining the Feminization of Teaching in the Nineteenth Century with Emphasis on the Displaced Male Teacher." Senior independent study thesis, paper 3816, 2012. https://openworks.wooster.edu/independent-study/3816

Ford, Gerald. Interview on CBS's *Face the Nation* by George Herman.. CBS News, June 6, 1976. https://www.presidency.ucsb.edu/documents/interview-cbs-news-face-the-nation

Frankenberg, Erica, and Gary Orfield, eds. *The Resegregation of Suburban Schools: A Hidden Crisis in American Schools*. Cambridge: Harvard Educational Press, 2012.

Frankenberg, Erica, Jongyeon Ee, Jennifer B. Ayscue, and Gary Orfield. *Harming Our Common Future: America's Segregated Schools 65 Years after Brown*. Los Angeles: UCLA Civil Rights Project, 2019. Accessed October 20, 2019. https://www.civilrightsproject.ucla.edu/research/k-12-education/integration-and-diversity/harming-our-common-future-americas-segregated-schools-65-years-after-brown/Brown-65–050919v4-final.pdf

Franklin, Benjamin. "A Proposal for Promoting Useful Knowledge, 14 May 1743." *Founders Online*, National Archives, accessed September 29, 2019. https://founders.archives.gov/documents/Franklin/01-02-02-0092

Franklin, Benjamin. "Proposals Relating to the Education of Youth in Pennsylvania (October 1749)." *Founders Online*, National Archives. Accessed September 29, 2019. https://founders.archives.gov/documents/Franklin/01-03-02-0166

Freeman v. Pitts. Oyez. Accessed October 20, 2019. https://www.oyez.org/cases/1991/89–1290.

Frum, David. *How We Got Here: The '70s*. New York: Basic Books, 2000.

Gay, Geneva. *Culturally Responsive Teaching: Theory, Research, and Practice*. New York: Teachers College Press, 2018.

Gill, Brian P. "Charter Schools and Segregation, What the Research Says." EducationNext,

November 19, 2018. https://www.educationnext.org/charter-schools-segrega
tion-what-research-says/

Genovese, Michael A. *The Nixon Presidency: Power and Politics in Turbulent Times.* New
York: Praeger, 1990.

Goldstein, Dana. "Obama Education Rules Are Swept Aside by Congress." *New York
Times*, March 10, 2017. https://www.nytimes.com/2017/03/09/us/every-student-
succeeds-act-essa-congress.html?_r=0

Government Accountability Office. *K-12 Education: Better Use of Information Could Help
Agencies Identify Disparities and Address Racial Discrimination.* Washington, D.C.:
Government Accountability Office, 2016. Accessed October 20, 2019. http://www.
gao.gov/assets/680/676745.pdf

Hammond, Zaretta. *Culturally Responsive Teaching and the Brain: Promoting Authentic
Engagement and Rigor among Culturally and Linguistically Diverse Students.* Thousand Oaks, Calif.: Corwin, 2015.

Hanna-Jones, Nikole. "School Districts Still Face Fights—and Confusion—on Integration."
Atlantic, May 2, 2014. http://www.theatlantic.com/education/archive/2014/05/lack-
of-order-the-erosion-of-a-once-great-force-for-integration/361563

Hansen, Michael, Elizabeth Mann Levesque, Diana Quintero, and Jon Valant. "Have We
Made Progress on Achievement Gaps? Looking at Evidence from the New NAEP
Results." Brookings, April 17, 2018. https://www.brookings.edu/blog/brown-cen
ter-chalkboard/2018/04/17/have-we-made-progress-on-achievement-gaps-looking-
at-evidence-from-the-new-naep-results/

Heller, Celia Stopnicka. *Structured Social Inequality: A Reader in Comparative Social
Stratification.* 2nd ed. New York: Macmillan, 1987.

Herbert, Bob. "Impossible, Ridiculous, Repugnant." *New York Times*, October 6, 2005.
https://www.nytimes.com/2005/10/06/opinion/impossible-ridiculous-repugnant.
html

Herbert, Bob. "Righting Reagan's Wrongs?" *New York Times*, November 13, 2007. http://
www.nytimes.com/2007/11/13/opinion/13herbert.html?_r=1

Hersh, Seymour. *The Price of Power: Kissinger in the Nixon White House.* New York:
Summit Books, 1983.

Hervani, Aref, Marilyn Helms, Raina Rutti, Joanne LaBonte, and Sy Sarkarat. "Service
Learning Projects in Online Courses: Delivery Strategies." *Journal of Learning in
Higher Education* 11, no. 1 (2015): 35–41.

Heyrman, Christine Leigh. *Southern Cross: The Beginnings of the Bible Belt.* Chapel Hill:
University of North Carolina Press, 1998.

Highsmith, Andrew R. *Demolition Means Progress: Flint, Michigan and the Fate of the
American Metropolis.* Chicago: University of Chicago Press, 2015.

Highsmith, Andrew R., and Ansley T. Erickson. "Segregation as Splitting, Segregation as
Joining: Schools, Housing, and the Many Modes of Jim Crow." *American Journal of
Education* 121, no. 4 (August 2015): 563–95.

Hirsch, Arnold. R. *Making the Second Ghetto: Race and Housing in Chicago, 1940–1960.*
Chicago: University of Chicago Press, 1983.

Howard, Tyrone C. *Why Race and Culture Matter in Schools: Closing the Achievement Gap in America's Classrooms.* New York: Teachers College Press, 2010.

Humphrey, Hubert H. "1948 Democratic National Convention Address." Speech presented at the 1948 Democratic National Convention, Philadelphia, July 14, 1948. American Rhetoric. http://www.americanrhetoric.com/speeches/huberthumphey 1948dnc.html

Hyland, Nora E. "Detracking in Social Studies: A Path to a More Democratic Education?" *Theory into Practice* 45, no. 1 (2006): 64–71.

Indiana Historical Society. "Indiana Public Schools Desegregation Case Collection, 1971–1999." Indianapolis: Indiana Historical Society. http://www.indianahistory.org/our-collections/collection-guides/indianapolis-public-schools-desegregation-case.pdf

Jackson, Marissa. "Neo-Colonialism, Same Old Racism: A Critical Analysis of the United States' Shift toward Colorblindness as a Tool for the Protection of the American Colonial Empire and White Supremacy." *Berkeley Journal of African-American Law and Policy* 11, no. 1 (2009): 156–91.

James Edward T., ed. *The Dictionary of American Biography, Supplement Three: 1941–1945.* New York: Charles Scribner's Sons, 1974.

Jefferson Thomas. "The Letters of Thomas Jefferson: 1743–1826." American History from Revolution to Reconstruction, and Beyond. http://www.let.rug.nl/usa/presidents/thomas-jefferson/letters-of-thomas-jefferson/

Jefferson, Thomas. "Notes on the State of Virginia, Query XVIII: Manners." 1781. Teaching American History. https://teachingamericanhistory.org/library/document/notes-on-the-state-of-virginia-query-xviii-manners/

Jefferson, Thomas. "Notes on the State of Virginia." 1787. Avalon Project: Yale Law School. http://www.gutenberg.org/files/56313/56313-h/56313-h.htm

Jefferson, Thomas. "Thomas Jefferson to Charles Yancy, Monticello, VA, January 6, 1816." *Founders Online.* National Archives. Accessed October 15, 2019. https://founders.archives.gov/documents/Jefferson/03-09-02-0209

Jefferson, Thomas. "Thomas Jefferson to John Lynch, Monticello, VA, January 21, 1811." *Founders Online.* National Archives. Accessed October 15, 2019. https://founders.archives.gov/documents/Jefferson/03-03-02-0243

Jefferson, Thomas. "Thomas Jefferson to Peter Carr, Monticello, VA, September 7, 1814." Accessed October 15, 2019. https://www.encyclopediavirginia.org/Letter_from_Thomas_Jefferson_to_Peter_Carr_September_7_1814

Johnson, Lyndon B. "Johnson's Remarks on Signing the Elementary and Secondary Act." Speech Presented at Johnson City, Texas, April 11, 1965. LBJ Presidential Library. http://www.lbjlibrary.org/lyndon-baines-johnson/timeline/johnsons-remarks-on-signing-the-elementary-and-secondary-education-act

Johnson, Rucker C. "Long-Run Impacts of School Desegregation and School Quality on Adult Attainments." NBER Working Paper No. 16664, January 2011, revised August 2015. Cambridge: National Bureau of Economic Research. https://gsppi.berkeley.edu/~ruckerj/johnson_schooldesegregation_NBERw16664.pdf

Keller, Bess. "Stanford Professor Created a New Breed of Professional." *Education Week* 19, no. 12 (1999): 1–4.

Kendi, Ibram X. *Stamped from the Beginning: The Definitive History of Racist Ideas in America.* New York: Nation Books, 2016.

Kerbo, Harold R. *Social Stratification and Inequality: Class Conflict in Historical and Comparative Perspective.* 8th ed. New York: McGraw-Hill, 2012.

Khan, Azmat. "The Republicans' Plan for the New President." *Frontline*, Public Broadcast System, January 15, 2013. http://www.pbs.org/wgbh/frontline/article/the-republi cans-plan-for-the-new-president/

Kim, Myungsung. "Afrofuturism, Science Fiction, and the Reinvention of African American Culture." PhD diss., Arizona State University, 2017. https://repository.asu.edu/ attachments/189587/content/Kim_asu_0010E_17187.pdf

King, Martin L. "I Have a Dream." Speech presented at the March on Washington for Jobs and Freedom, Washington, D.C., August 1968. http://avalon.law.yale.edu/20th_cen tury/mlk01.asp

Kite, Mary K. "Multicultural Competence: Engaging in Difficult Dialogues That Are Inherent in Teaching about Diversity." American Psychological Association. Accessed October 20, 2019. https://www.apa.org/ed/precollege/ptn/2015/02/multicultur al-competence

Klein, Alyson. "How Workable Is Trump's $20 Billion School Choice Proposal?" *Education Week*, November 17, 2016. http://blogs.edweek.org/edweek/campaign-k-12/2016/11/ trump_20_billion_school_choice_plan.html

Klein, Alyson. "What Have the Presidential Candidates Said about School Integration?" *Education Week*, October 31, 2016. http://blogs.edweek.org/edweek/cam paign-k-12/2016/10/what_have_the_presidential_can.html

Kozol, Johnathan. *Savage Inequalities: Children in America's Schools.* New York: Harper Perennial, 1991.

Kozol, Jonathan, Beverly Daniel Tatum, Susan Eaton, and Patricia Gándara. "Resegregation: What's the Answer?" *Educational Leadership* 68, no. 3 (2010): 28–31. Accessed October 20, 2019. http://www.ascd.org/publications/educational-leadership/nov10/ vol68/num03/Resegregation@-What's-the-Answer%C2%A2.aspx

Labaree, David F. *Someone Has to Fail: The Zero-Sum Game of Public Schooling.* Cambridge: Harvard University Press, 2010.

Lamis, Alexander P. *The Two Party South.* Oxford: Oxford University Press, 1990.

Lane, Barbara M. "Construction of the Racist Republican." Thesis, Georgia State University, 2014. https://scholarworks.gsu.edu/history_theses/81

Loewus, Liana. "The Nation's Teaching Force Is Still Mostly White and Female." *Education Week*, August 15, 2017. https://www.edweek.org/ew/articles/2017/08/15/the-nations-teaching-force-is-still-mostly.html

Lydon, Christopher. "Carter Defends All White Areas." *New York Times*, April 7, 1976. http://www.nytimes.com/1976/04/07/archives/carter-defends-allwhite-areas-says-government-shouldnt-try-to-end.html?_r=0

Maclure, William. *Opinions on Various Subjects Dedicated to the Industrious Producers.* New Harmony: School Press, 1831.

Mantil, Ann, Anne G. Perkins, and Stephanie Aberger. "The Challenge of High-Poverty Schools: How Feasible Is Socioeconomic School Integration?" In *The Future of*

School Integration, edited by Richard D. Kahlenberg. New York: Century Foundation, 2012.

Marshall, Thurgood. "*Milliken v. Bradley*/Dissent Marshall." https://en.wikisource.org/wiki/Milliken_v._Bradley/Dissent_Marshall

McAndrews, Lawrence J. "Missing the Bus: Gerald Ford and School Desegregation." *Presidential Studies Quarterly* 99, no. 4 (1997): 791–804.

McAndrews, Lawrence J. "Not the Bus, but Us: George W. Bush and School Desegregation." *Education Foundations* (Winter–Spring 2009): 67–82.

McAndrews, Lawrence J. "Talking the Talk: Bill Clinton and School Desegregation." *International Social Science Review*, September 22, 2004. https://www.thefreelibrary.com/Talking+the+talk%3A+Bill+Clinton+and+school+desegregation.-a0128168183

McCord, David J., ed. *The Statutes at Large of South Carolina. Vol. 7, Containing the Acts Relating to Charleston, Courts, Slaves, and Rivers*. Columbia: A.S. Johnston, 1840.

Mehta, Seema, and Michael Finnegan. "Segregation Has Soared in America's Schools as Federal Leaders Largely Looked Away." *Los Angeles Times*, July 8, 2019. https://www.latimes.com/politics/la-na-pol-2020-school-segregation-busing-harris-biden-20190708-story.html

Metzger, Molly, and Henry Webber. *Facing Segregation: Housing Policy Solutions for a Stronger Society*. Oxford: Oxford University Press, 2018.

Middlecamp, David. "Getting Fired by Nixon Turned Out Pretty Well for Leon Panetta." *Tribune* (San Luis Obispo, Calif.), May 12, 2017. https://www.sanluisobispo.com/news/local/news-columns-blogs/photos-from-the-vault/article150282472.html

Milliken v. Bradley, 418 U.S. 717 (1974). Accessed October 20, 2019. https://supreme.justia.com/cases/federal/us/418/717/case.html

Mondale, Sarah, and Sarah B. Patton, eds. *School: The Story of American Public Education*. Boston: Beacon Press, 2001.

Moses, Michele S., and Michael J. Nanna. "The Testing Culture and the Persistence of High Stakes Testing Reforms." *E&C/Education and Culture* 23, no. 1 (2007): 55–72.

Moss, Hilary J. *Schooling Citizens: The Struggle for African American Education in Antebellum America*. Chicago: University of Chicago Press, 2009.

Nash, Margaret. *Women's Education in the United States, 1780–1840*. New York: Palgrave Macmillan, 2005.

National Education Association. *Report of the Committee of Ten on Secondary School Studies*. New York: American Book Co, 1894.

Neem, Johann N. *Democracy's Schools: The Rise of Public Education in America (How Things Worked)*. Baltimore: Johns Hopkins University Press, 2017.

Neftali, Tim. "Ronald Reagan's Long Hidden Racist Conversation with Richard Nixon." *Atlantic*, July 30, 2019. https://www.theatlantic.com/ideas/archive/2019/07/ronald-reagans-racist-conversation-richard-nixon/595102/

Neuberger, Thomas Stephen, and Thomas C. Crumplar. "Tax Exempt Religious Schools under Attack: Conflicting Goals of Religious Freedom and Racial Integration." 49 *Fordham Law Review* 229 (1980). http://ir.lawnet.fordham.edu/flr/vol49/iss3/1

Nixon, Richard M. "President Nixon on School Busing." April 29, 1971. Nixon Foundation. Accessed October 20, 2019. https://www.youtube.com/watch?v=7d8Zm9kl488

Nixon, Richard M. "Statement about Desegregation of Elementary and Secondary Schools." March 24, 1970. American Presidency Project. https://www.presidency.ucsb.edu/documents/statement-about-desegregation-elementary-and-second ary-schools

Nodjimbadem, Katie. "The Racial Segregation of American Cities Was Anything but Accidental: A Housing Policy Expert Explains How Federal Government Policies Created the Suburbs and the Inner City." *Smithsonian*, May 30, 2017. https://www.smithsonianmag.com/history/how-federal-government-intentionally-racially-segre gated-american-cities-180963494/

"Northwest Ordinance, July 13, 1787: An Ordinance for the Governing of the Territory of the United States Northwest of the River Ohio." Avalon Project at Yale University. Accessed September 16, 2019. https://avalon.law.yale.edu/18th_century/nworder.asp

Oakes, Jeannie. *Keeping Track: How Schools Structure Inequality.* New Haven: Yale University Press, 2005.

Obama, Barack H. "Remarks by the President at LBJ Presidential Library Civil Rights Summit." April 10, 2014. White House Office of the Press Secretary. https://obamawhitehouse.archives.gov/the-press-office/2014/04/10/remarks-presi dent-lbj-presidential-library-civil-rights-summit

Olsen, Skylar. "Black and White Homeownership Rate Gap Has Widened since 1900." Zillow, April 10, 2018. https://www.zillow.com/research/homeownership-gap-wid ens-19384/

O'Reilly, Kenneth. *Nixon's Piano: Presidents and Racial Politics from Washington to Clinton.* New York: Free Press, 1995.

Orfield, Gary. "Schools More Separate: Consequences of a Decade of Resegregation," Civil Rights Project. Cambridge: Harvard University, 2001. https://eric.ed.gov /?id=ED459217

Orfield, Gary, Erica Frankenberg, Jongyeon Ee, and John Kuscera. *Brown at 60: Great Progress, a Long Retreat, and an Uncertain Future.* Los Angeles: UCLA Civil Rights Project/Proyecto Derechos Civiles, 2014. https://www.civilrightsproject.ucla.edu/ research/k-12-education/integration-and-diversity/brown-at-60-great-progress-a-long-retreat-and-an-uncertain-future/Brown-at-60–051814.pdf

Orfield, Gary, Erica Frankenberg, Jongyeon Ee, and Genevieve Siegel-Hawley. *Brown at 62: School Segregation by Race, Poverty, and State.* Los Angeles: UCLA Civil Rights Project/Proyecto Derechos Civiles, 2016. https://www.civilrightsproject.ucla.edu/ research/k-12-education/integration-and-diversity/brown-at-62-school-segregation-by-race-poverty-and-state

Orr, Asaf, and Joel Baum. *Schools in Transition: A Guide for Supporting Transgender Students in K-12 Schools.* Washington, D.C.: Human Rights Campaign Foundation, 2015. https://www.genderspectrum.org/staging/wp-content/uploads/2015/08/ Schools-in-Transition-2015.pdf

Padover, Saul K. *Thomas Jefferson on Democracy.* New York: Appleton-Century Company, 1939.

Palvia, Shailendra, Prageet Aeron, Paul Gupta, Diptiranjan Mahapatra, Parida Ratri, Rebecca Rosner, and Sumita Sindhi. "Online Education: Worldwide Status, Challenges, Trends, and Implications." *Journal of Global Information Technology Management* 21, no. 4 (2018): 233–41. doi:10.1080/1097198X.2018.1542262.

Panetta, Leon, and Peter Gall. *Bring Us Together: The Nixon Team and the Civil Rights Retreat.* Philadelphia: J. B. Lippincott, 1971.

Parents Involved in Community Schools v. Seattle School District No. 1. Oyez. Accessed October 20, 2019. https://www.oyez.org/cases/2006/05–908

Paris, Django, and H. Samy Alim, eds. *Culturally Sustaining Pedagogies: Teaching and Learning for Justice in a Changing World.* New York: Teachers College Press, 2017.

Perlstein, Daniel. "Class." In *Miseducation: A History of Ignorance-Making in America and Abroad*, edited by A. J. Angulo, 125–39. Baltimore: John Hopkins University Press, 2016.

Phillips, Kevin. *Bill Moyer's Journal*, interview. Public Broadcasting System, November 7, 2008. http://www.pbs.org/moyers/journal/11072008/watch3.html

Phillips, Kevin. *The Emerging Republican Majority.* New York: Arlington House, 1969.

Plessy v. Ferguson. Cornell Law School, Legal Information Institute. Accessed October 20, 2019. http://straylight.law.cornell.edu/supct/html/historics/USSC_CR_0163_0537_ZO.html

Pontin, Jason. "The Importance of Feelings." *MIT Technology Review*, June 17, 2014. https://www.technologyreview.com/s/528151/the-importance-of-feelings/

Pratt, Richard H. "The Advantages of Mingling Indians with Whites." 1892. In *Americanizing the American Indians: Writings by the "Friends of the Indian," 1880–1900*, edited by Francis Paul Prucha. Cambridge: Harvard University Press, 1973.

Ranganathan, Srinthya, Solomon Negash, and Marlene Wilcox. 2007. "Hybrid Learning: Balancing Face-to-Face and Online Class Sessions." *Proceedings of the 2007 Southern Association for Information Systems Conference*, 178–82. http://citeseerx.ist.psu.edu/viewdoc/download?doi=10.1.1.489.2130&rep=rep1&type=pdf

Ravitch, Diane. "American Traditions in Education." In *A Primer on America's Schools*, edited by Terry M. Moe. Stanford: Hoover Institution Press, 2001.

Ravitch, Diane. *Left Back: A Century of Battles over School Reforms.* New York: Simon and Schuster, 2001.

Reardon, Sean F. 2016. "School Segregation and Racial Academic Achievement Gaps." Paper prepared for the Russell Sage Foundation Conference, "The Coleman Report at Fifty: Its Legacy and Enduring Value." http://blogs.edweek.org/edweek/inside-school-research/reardon%20segregation%20and%20achievement%20gaps%20apr2016.pdf

Reardon, Sean F., Demetra Kalogrides, and Kenneth Shores. "The Geography of Racial/Ethnic Test Score Gaps." *American Journal of Sociology* 124, no. 4 (January 2019): 1164–1221. Accessed October 20, 2019. https://www.journals.uchicago.edu/doi/abs/10.1086/700678

Rotberg, Iris C. "Backtalk: The Social Costs of Proliferating Charter Schools." *Phi Delta Kappan* 100, no. 7 (2019): 80.

Rothstein, Richard. *The Color of Law: A Forgotten History of How Our Government Segregated America.* Brown University, January 24, 2019. video, 49 minutes. https://www.youtube.com/watch?v=r9UqnQC7jY4

Rothstein, Richard. "The Racial Achievement Gap, Segregated Schools, and Segregated Neighborhoods—a Constitutional Insult." Economic Policy Institute, November 12, 2014. https://www.epi.org/publication/the-racial-achievement-gap-segregated-schools-and-segregated-neighborhoods-a-constitutional-insult/

Rothstein, Richard, and Mark Santow. "A Different Kind of Choice: Educational Inequality and the Continuing Significance of Racial Segregation." Economic Policy Institute, August 21, 2012. https://archive.org/stream/ERIC_ED537326/ERIC_ED537326_djvu.txt

"Rudyard Kipling: 1965–1936." Accessed October 26, 2005. http://www.kipling.org.uk/kip_fra.htm

Rusher, William A. "Crossroads for the GOP." *National Review,* February 12, 1963. Accessed September 15, 2012. http://www.unz.org/Pub/National-Rev-1963feb12–00109

Russell, Garnett. "Race and Cultural Flexibility among Students in Different Multiracial Schools." Stanford University Graduate School of Education: News Center. Accessed October 1, 2019. https://ed.stanford.edu/spotlight/cultural-hurdles-achieving-school-integration

Ryan, Mark. *Ask the Teacher: A Practitioner's Guide to Teaching and Learning in the Diverse Classroom.* Boston: Allyn and Bacon, 2008.

Ryan, Mark. "The Enduring Legacy: Structured Inequality in America's Public Schools." *Canyon Journal of Interdisciplinary Studies* 5, no. 2 (2016): 66–84.

Sack, Kevin. "In Little Rock, Clinton Warns of Racial Split." *New York Times*, September 26, 1997. http://www.nytimes.com/1997/09/26/us/in-little-rock-clinton-warns-of-racial-split.html

"SAT Math Scores Hit 30-Year High." *CNN* online, August 27, 2002. http://edition.cnn.com/2002/fyi/teachers.ednews/08/27/sat.scores/

Schugurensky, Daniel. "History of Education: Selected Moments of the Twentieth Century." Accessed October 2, 2019. http://schugurensky.faculty.asu.edu/moments/1965elemsec.html

Scott, Daryl Michael. *Contempt and Pity: Social Policy and the Image of the Damaged Black Psyche, 1880–1996.* Chapel Hill: University of North Carolina Press, 1997.

"Segregated Neighborhoods, Segregated Schools?" Urban Institute, November 28, 2018. https://www.urban.org/features/segregated-neighborhoods-segregated-schools

"Separate Is Not Equal: *Brown v. Board of Education.*" Smithsonian Institution. Accessed October 20, 2019. http://americanhistory.si.edu/brown/history/6-legacy/deliberate-speed.html

Shields, Mark. "The 'Death' of the GOP." Creators Syndicate, July 2, 2016. http://www.creators.com/read/mark-shields/07/16/the-death-of-the-gop

Silver, Nate. "GOP Has Always Been Dominated by White Voters." FiveThirtyEight, July 1, 2009. http://fivethirtyeight.com/features/gop-has-always-been-dominated-by-white/

Smith, Alan. "Trump Says Congresswomen of Color Should 'Go Back' and Fix the Places They 'Originally Came From.'" *NBC News*, July 14, 2019. https://www.nbcnews.com/politics/donald-trump/trump-says-progressive-congresswomen-should-go-back-where-they-came-n1029676

Smith, Peter. "From Scarcity to Abundance: IT's Role in Achieving Quality-Assured Mass Higher Education." *Journal of Asynchronous Learning Networks* 15, no. 2 (Spring 2011): 8–12. https://files.eric.ed.gov/fulltext/EJ935573.pdf

Smith, Peter. *Harnessing America's Wasted Talent: A New Ecology of Learning.* San Francisco: Jossey-Bass, 2010.

Solberg, Carl. *Hubert Humphrey: A Biography.* St. Paul: Minnesota Historical Society Press, 2003.

Spring, Joel. *Conflicts of Interests: The Politics of American Education.* New York: Longman, 1993.

Stevenson, Adlai. "Address to the Citizens' School Committee, Chicago, Illinois." 1948. Accessed October 15, 2019. http://adlaitoday.org/ideas/quotes_care.html

Stewart, Vivien. "A Classroom as Wide as the World." In *Curriculum 21: Essential Education for a Changing World*, edited by H. H. Jacobs. Alexandria: ASCD, 2010.

Theoharis, George. "'Forced Busing' Didn't Fail: Desegregation Is the Best Way to Improve Our Schools." *Washington Post*, October 23, 2015. https://www.washingtonpost.com/posteverything/wp/2015/10/23/forced-busing-didnt-fail-desegregation-is-the-best-way-to-improve-our-schools/?utm_term=.32c4caf44d00

Thomas Jefferson Foundation. "VI. Conclusions: Report of the Research Committee on Thomas Jefferson and Sally Hemings." Charlottesville, Va.: Thomas Jefferson Foundation. https://www.monticello.org/site/plantation-and-slavery/vi-conclusions

Thompson, Chalmer E., and Robert T. Carter, eds. *Racial Identity Theory: Applications to Individual, Group, and Organizational Interventions.* New York: Routledge, 2012.

Thurber, Timothy N. "Goldwaterism Triumphant? Race and the Republican Party, 1965–1968." *Journal of the Historical Society* 7, no. 3 (September 2007): 349–84. https://doi.org/10.1111/j.1540–5923.2007.00221.x

Tix, Andy. "Improving the Experience of Online Education." *Psychology Today*, November 28, 2016. https://www.psychologytoday.com/us/blog/the-pursuit-peace/201611/improving-the-experience-online-education

Tolley, Kimberly. *Heading South to Teach: The World of Susan Nye Hutchison, 1815–1845.* Chapel Hill: University of North Carolina Press, 2015.

Tolley, Kimberly. "Slavery." In *Miseducation: A History of Ignorance-Making in America and Abroad*, edited by A. J. Angulo, 13–33. Baltimore: John Hopkins University Press, 2016.

Totenberg, Nina. "Heated Arguments Fly at Supreme Court over Race in College Admissions." *All Things Considered.* National Public Radio, December 9, 2015. http://www.npr.org/2015/12/09/459099492/supreme-court-revisits-affirmative-action-in-higher-education

Trounstine, Jessica. *Segregation by Design: Local Politics and Inequality in American Cities.* Cambridge: Cambridge University Press, 2018.

Trump, Donald J. "Remarks by President Trump in Joint Address to Congress." White House Press Office, February 28, 2017. https://www.whitehouse.gov/briefings-statements/remarks-president-trump-joint-address-congress/

Trump, Donald J. "State of the Union." February 4, 2020. https://www.nytimes.com/2020/02/05/us/politics/state-of-union-transcript.html

"Trump Judicial Nominees and *Brown v. Board of Education*." *Weekend Edition*. National
     Public Radio, May 19, 2019. https://www.npr.org/2019/05/19/724747911/trump-
     judicial-nominees-and-brown-v-board-of-education
"Trump to Nominate 'Strict Constructionist' to Supreme Court: Pence." Reuters, January
     26, 2017. https://www.reuters.com/article/us-usa-court-pence-idUSKBN15A2RR
Tyack, David. "Democracy in Education—Who Needs it?" *Editorial Projects in Education*
     19, no. 12 (1999): 42.
Tyack, David, and Larry Cuban. *Tinkering with Utopia: A Century of Public School
     Reform*. 6th ed. Cambridge: Harvard University Press, 2003.
U.S. Census Bureau. "New Census Bureau Report Analyzes U.S. Population Projec-
     tions." News release, March 3, 2015. https://www.census.gov/newsroom/press-re-
     leases/2015/cb15-tps16.html
U.S. Census Bureau. "Quickfacts." Accessed July 5, 2016. http://quickfacts.census.gov
Valencia, Richard, ed. *The Evolution of Deficit Thinking: Educational Thought and Prac-
     tice*. London: RoutledgeFalmer, 1997.
Warner, Charles Dudley. "The Education of the Negro." 1900. Project Gutenberg.
     Accessed September 19, 2019. http://www.gutenberg.org/dirs/3/1/1/3114/3114.txt
Weinraub, Bernard. "Burger Retiring, Rehnquist Named Chief; Scalia, Appeals
     Judge, Chosen for Court." *New York Times*, June 18, 1986. https://www.nytimes.
     com/1986/06/18/us/burger-retiring-rehnquist-named-chief-scalia-appeals-judge-
     chosen-for-court.html
Weiss, Debra Cassens. "Kavanaugh Lands in Top Six in 'Scalia-ness' Ranking of SCOTUS
     Contenders; Who Is No. 1?" *ABA Journal*, January 16, 2018. http://www.abajournal.
     com/news/article/kavanaugh_lands_in_top_six_in_scalia_ness_ranking_of_scotus
     _contenders_who
Wells, Amy Stuart, Lauren Fox, and Diana Cordova-Cobo. "How Racially Diverse Schools
     and Classrooms Can Benefit All Students." Century Foundation, February 9, 2016.
     https://tcf.org/content/report/how-racially-diverse-schools-and-classrooms-can-
     benefit-all-students/
Wells, Amy Stuart, Jennifer J. Holme, Awo K. Atanda, and Anita T. Revilla. "Tackling
     Racial Segregation One Policy at a Time: Why School Desegregation Only Went
     So Far." *Teachers College Record* 107 no. 9 (September 2005): 2141–77. https://eric.
     ed.gov/?id=EJ718517
Wells, Amy Stuart, Jennifer Holme, Anita T. Revilla, and Awo K. Atanda. *How Desegre-
     gation Changed Us: The Effects of Racially Mixed Schools on Students and Society, a
     Study of Desegregated High Schools and Their Class of 1980 Graduates*. New York:
     Teachers College, Columbia University, 2004. https://www.tc.columbia.edu/faculty/
     asw86/faculty-profile/files/ASWells041504.pdf
Williams, Juan. "Reagan Blames Courts for Education Decline." *Washington Post*, June 30,
     1983. https://www.washingtonpost.com/archive/politics/1983/06/30/reagan-blames-
     courts-for-education-decline/729b84ac-d6de-4abb-b628-21d6b6b4e872/
Williams, Juan. "Reagan, the South, and Civil Rights." *Politically Speaking*. National Public
     Radio, June 10, 2004. http://www.npr.org/templates/story/story.php?storyId=1953700
Yoakum, Clarence S., and Robert Means Yerkes, eds. *Army Mental Tests*. New York:
     Henry Holt and Company, 1920.

Zadra, Jonathan, and Gerald Clore. "Emotion and Perception: The Role of Affective Information." *Wiley Interdisciplinary Reviews of Cognitive Science* 2, no. 6
(November–December 2001): 676–685. https://www.ncbi.nlm.nih.gov/pmc/articles/
PMC3203022/
Zhang, Catharine. "The State of Integration in the United States." *Harvard Political
Review*, September 9, 2016. http://harvardpolitics.com/united-states/state-integra
tion-united-states/

IMAGE CREDITS

Figure 1. San Francisco, Calif., April 1942. *Children at the Weill Public School for the So-called International Settlement and Including Many Japanese-Americans, Saluting the Flag. They Include Evacuees of Japanese Descent Who Will be Housed in War Relocation Authority Centers for the Duration.* San Francisco, California, April 1942. Photograph. Library of Congress. https://www.loc.gov/item/2001705928/

Figure 2. George Edward Perine, Engraver, and Charles Nicolas Cochin. *Benj. Franklin / Engraved by Geo. E. Perine, N.Y., for the Eclectic, after Drawing by C.N. Cochin.* Undated [between 1860 and 1885] Engraving. https://www.loc.gov/item/2005693049/

Figure 3. Charles Balthazar Julien Fevret De Saint-Mémin, Artist. *Thomas Jefferson, Head-and-Shoulders Portrait, Facing Right.* 1805. Washington, D.C. Engraving. Library of Congress. https://www.loc.gov/item/97503644/

Figure 4. Thomas Nast. *Our Common Schools As They Are And As They May Be.* 1870. Wood Engraving. In Harper's Weekly, February 26, 1870, 140. Library of Congress. https://www.loc.gov/pictures/resource/cph.3b33478/

Figure 5. Frances Benjamin Johnston. *School Children of the Sixth Division in a Horse Drawn Car.* Washington, D.C. 1899? Photograph. Library of Congress. https://www.loc.gov/pictures/resource/cph.3a16943/

Figure 6. Lewis Wickes Hine. *Immigrants in Night School.* Boston. October 1909. Photograph. Library of Congress. https://www.loc.gov/pictures/resource/nclc.04549/

Figure 7. Branches Benjamin Johnston. *African American Schoolgirls with Teacher, Learning to Cook on a Wood Stove in Classroom.* Washington, D.C. 1899? Photograph. Library of Congress. https://www.loc.gov/item/2001699122/

Figure 8. George Crofutt. *American Progress.* 1873. Chromolithograph; painting by John Gast. Library of Congress. https://www.loc.gov/item/97507547/

Figure 9. Frances Benjamin Johnston. *Washington, D.C. Public School Classroom Scenes—1st Division Geography Class—Students Examining Relief Map.* Washington, D.C. 1899? Photograph. Library of Congress. https://www.loc.gov/item/2001703689/

Figure 10. George Prince. *Theodore Roosevelt Portrait, Facing Front.* July 14, 1904. Photograph. Library of Congress. https://www.loc.gov/item/2013649835/

Figure 11. Louis Dalrymple. *School Begins.* Chromolithograph. In *Puck* 144, no. 1142. Library of Congress. https://www.loc.gov/pictures/resource/ppmsca.28668/

Figure 12. *American Education.* 1943. Photograph. Library of Congress. https://www.loc.gov/pictures/resource/cph.3c32028/?co=fsa

Figure 13. Thomas O'Halloran. *School Integration. Barnard School, Washington, D.C.* Washington, D.C. May 27, 1955. Photograph. Library of Congress. https://www.loc.gov/item/2003654384/

Figure 14. Marion S. Trikosko. *Civil Rights Leaders Meet with President John F. Kennedy in the Oval Office of the White House after the March on Washington, D.C.* Washington, D.C. August 28, 1963. Photograph. Library of Congress. https://www.loc.gov/item/2013648833/

Figure 15. Warren K. Leffler. *Ku Klux Klan Members Supporting Barry Goldwater's Campaign for the Presidential Nomination at the Republican National Convention, San Francisco, California, as an African American Man Pushes Signs Back.* San Francisco. July 12, 1964. Photograph. Library of Congress. https://www.loc.gov/item/2003673964/

Figure 16. Warren K. Leffler. *Pres. Richard Nixon Tossing Out Baseball at Senators' Opening Game with New York, Washington, D.C.* Washington, D.C. April 7, 1969. Photograph. Library of Congress. https://www.loc.gov/item/93500527/

Figure 17. Warren K. Leffler. *Governor George Wallace Attempting to Block Integration at the University of Alabama.* Tuscaloosa. June 11, 1963. Photograph. Library of Congress. https://www.loc.gov/item/2003688161/

Figure 18. Warren K. Leffler. *African American and White School Children on a School Bus, Riding from the Suburbs to an Inner City School, Charlotte, North Carolina.* Charlotte. February 21, 1973. Photograph Library of Congress. https://www.loc.gov/item/2011648709/

Figure 19. Thomas O'Halloran. *President Gerald Ford Makes a Victory Sign as George Wallace Applauds at a Campaign Stop in the South.* September 1976. Photograph. Library of Congress. https://www.loc.gov/pictures/resource/ppmsca.08527/

Figure 20. Warren K. Leffler. *Jimmy Carter and Sen. Hubert Humphrey at the Democratic National Convention, New York City, July 15, 1976.* Photograph. Library of Congress. https://www.loc.gov/pictures/resource/ppmsca.09737/

Figure 21. Carol M. Highsmith. *President Ronald Reagan at His Desk in the White House Oval Office, Washington, D.C.* Washington, D.C. Photograph. Library of Congress. https://www.loc.gov/pictures/resource/highsm.18335/

Figure 22. Maureen Keating. *Senator Bob Dole and Senator Chris Dodd Present a Large "Speech Report Card" Marked With an A+ to President George H.W. Bush.* Washington, D.C. January 29, 1992. Photograph. Library of Congress. https://www.loc.gov/pictures/resource/ppmsca.38839/

Figure 23. Warren K. Leffler. *Senator Thurmond of South Carolina.* August 8, 1961. Photograph. Library of Congress. https://www.loc.gov/pictures/resource/ppmsca.19604/

Figure 24. *Bill Clinton, Half-Length Portrait, Seated at Desk, Facing Left.* Washington, D.C. 1993. Photograph. Library of Congress. https://www.loc.gov/pictures/resource/cph.3c24945/

Figure 25. Eric Draper. *Official Portrait of President George W. Bush.* Washington, D.C. 2003. Photograph. Library of Congress. https://www.loc.gov/pictures/resource/ppbd.00371/

Figure 26. Pete Souza. *Official Portrait of President-Elect Barack Obama.* Washington, D.C. January 13, 2009. Photograph. Library of Congress. https://www.loc.gov/pictures/resource/ppbd.00358/

Figure 27. Shealah Craighead. *Official Portrait of President Donald J. Trump.* Washington, D.C. October 6, 2017. Photograph. Library of Congress. https://www.loc.gov/pictures/resource/ppbd.00608/

Figure 28. Robert Butts. *Grayscale Photography of a Boy.* Santiago de los Caballeros, Dominican Republic. https://www.pexels.com/photo/grayscale-photography-of-boy-1330880/

Figure 29. Pixabay. *Boy Standing Near Bookshelf.* September 29, 2013. https://www.pexels.com/photo/adorable-blur-bookcase-books-261895/

Figure 30. Pixabay. *Person Coloring Art with Crayons.* June 7, 2016. https://www.pexels.com/photo/arts-and-crafts-child-close-up-color-159579/

Figure 31. Pixabay. *Girls Wearing Green and Gray Dress on Green Grass.* September 9, 2006. https://www.pexels.com/photo/action-adorable-athletes-boots-207739/

Figure 32. Mentatdgt. *Woman Sitting on Gray Chair.* https://www.pexels.com/photo/woman-sitting-on-gray-chair-1543895/

Figure 33. Karsten Madsen. *Macbook Pro Near iPhone and Apple Fruit.* October 30, 2015. https://www.pexels.com/photo/laptop-macbook-pro-office-computer-18105/

Figure 34. Zun Zun. *Group of People Forming Star Using Their Hands.* May 21, 2018. https://www.pexels.com/photo/group-of-people-forming-star-using-their-hands-1116302/

INDEX

Note: Page numbers in italics refer to the illustrations.

ability grouping. *See* tracking
accountability, school, 80, 99
achievement gap, 8, 83, 93–94, 96–99
affective benefits of integration, 99–101
affective domain and learning, 111–12
affirmative action, 42, 47–48, 73, 74
African Americans: antiliteracy laws,
    6–7, 51; "civilizing" of, 13; educators,
    10, 19–20; home ownership rates, 92;
    net worth, 92; nineteenth-century
    education, 10, 19; pedagogic benefits of
    integration, 96–98
Agnew, Spiro, 84
Alito, Samuel, 48, 75
American exceptionalism, 12, 27
American identity: and assimilation, 24–
    25, 30–31, 36; Columbia, *21*; develop-
    ment of, 10–12
American Independent Party, 58
Anglo-Saxon superiority, 23–24, 27, 28–32
anti-German sentiment, 25
antiliteracy laws, 6–7, 51
apartheid, South African, 65
apartheid of American schools. *See* reseg-
    regation
aptitude tests. *See* intelligence tests; SAT
    (Scholastic Aptitude Test)
Asian students: pedagogic benefits of
    integration, 98
assimilation: in Cubberley, 32; role of
    schools in, 4, 15, 20–25, 36, 109; of
    Spanish-American War territories, 30–31
attendance: nineteenth century, 10, 15, 20
Atwater, Lee, 69–72

Bates College, 106
Beecher, Catharine, 13–14

bias, 107–8
Biden, Joe, 61, 64
bigotry, soft, 102
Bilingual Education Act, 54
"A Bill for the More General Diffusion of
    Knowledge" (Jefferson), 4, 42
The Birth of a Nation (1915), 43
Black Law of 1833 (Connecticut), 10
Board of Education of Oklahoma v. Dowell,
    45
Bob Jones University v. United States,
    66–67
brain and learning, 111–12
Breyer, Stephen, 48
A Brief History of Education (Cubberley),
    27–30
Brigham, Carl, 34–35
Brown v. Board of Education of Topeka:
    district courts and, 84; Ford and, 63;
    history of, 44–46, 90; judicial nominees
    and, 42; Nixon and, 60; Panetta on, xi; as
    unenforced, 55, 85, 91
Brown v. Board of Education of Topeka II,
    84
Buckley, William F., 57
Burger, Warren E., 84
Bush, George Herbert Walker, 69–72
Bush, George W., 75, *76*, 80, 83
busing: Atwater on, 71–72; Biden on, 61,
    64; under Bush, George H. W., 72; under
    Carter, 64; Civil Rights Act of 1964, 52,
    55; Clinton's avoidance of, 74, 75; under
    Ford, 62–64; Humphrey on, 55; images,
    16, 60; McGovern on, 55–57; under
    Nixon, 59–62, 84; under Reagan, 68–69;
    Supreme Court on, 45, 46, 59–61; in
    twenty-first century, 104